COLONEL SANDERS AND THE AMERICAN DREAM

Discovering
AMERICA

Mark Crispin Miller, Series Editor

This series begins with a startling premise—that even now, more than two hundred years since its founding, America remains a largely undiscovered country with much of its amazing story yet to be told. In these books, some of America's foremost historians and cultural critics bring to light episodes in our nation's history that have never been explored. They offer fresh takes on events and people we thought we knew well and draw unexpected connections that deepen our understanding of our national character.

Josh Ozersky

COLONEL SANDERS
SANDERS
AND THE AMERICAN DREAM

University of Texas Press
AUSTIN

Requests for permission to reproduce material from this work should
be sent to:
    Permissions
    University of Texas Press
    P.O. Box 7819
    Austin, TX 78713-7819
    utpress.utexas.edu/rp-form

∞ The paper used in this book meets the minimum requirements of ANSI/
NISO Z39.48-1992 (R1997) (Permanence of Paper).

LIBRARY OF CONGRESS CATALOGING-IN-PUBLICATION DATA

Ozersky, Josh.
    Colonel Sanders and the American dream / Josh Ozersky. — 1st ed.
      p.   cm. — (Discovering America series)
    Includes index.
    ISBN 978-1-4773-1475-3 (pbk. : alk. paper)
    ISBN 978-0-292-74285-7 (e-book)
    1. Sanders, Harland, 1890–1980. 2. Restaurateurs—United States—
Biography. 3. Kentucky Fried Chicken (Firm)—History. I. Title.
    TX910.5.S25O95   2012

    647.95092—dc23 [B]   2011042865

[The Colonel]
was not only
our founder and
our creator,
he was our leader
and the driving force
behind KFC . . .
He was a
living example
that the
American Dream
still exists.

—Former Kentucky Fried Chicken president
JOHN Y. BROWN JR.
at Harland Sanders' funeral service

≡ CONTENTS ≡

≡ ACKNOWLEDGMENTS ≡

Any book needs help to be written, but this one needed more than most. I'd like to thank my editor at the University of Texas Press, the patient and encouraging Theresa J. May; my mentor and friend Mark Crispin Miller, who brought the book project into being; Rick Maynard at KFC, whose help was invaluable; Angela Collette, the best of friends, in Kentucky; John Y. Brown, the best of interview subjects, in the same lovely state; and most of all my wife, Danit Lidor, whose hard work, research, patience, love, and above all vigorous and incisive intellect contributed the most to this book. I owe every one of the above a bucket of Original Recipe, at the very least.

COLONEL SANDERS AND THE AMERICAN DREAM

Introduction

≡ HOW TO BECOME AN ICON ≡

Kentucky Fried Chicken got some alarming news in summer 2010. A survey commissioned by the company found that less than 40 percent of Americans ages eighteen to twenty-five were able to recognize Colonel Sanders, the chain's iconic founder, as a real person.[1] Now thirty years in the grave, the Colonel had, for a generation of KFC customers, simply ceased to exist as a human being. He was now a corporate avatar, a brand symbol like Aunt Jemima, Mrs. Butterworth, and the Morton Salt Girl. Worse still, from KFC's perspective, was the unmistakable inference to be drawn from these figures. If Colonel Sanders already seemed unreal to its customers after a single generation and in spite of the most strenuous efforts, what hope would it have of persuading future Americans to buy buckets? It was no abstract concern, a matter for the pondering of brand managers. There were a lot of chains in this country and overseas, and more all the time. They sold chicken too, and some of it was pretty good. The only thing separating KFC from them was the Colonel and whatever authority his image still conveyed.

Which was what? KFC didn't seem sure. In the thirty years since the Colonel's death, it had run headlong from his cooking methods, put an apron on him, taken it off, and even made him into a cartoon that sold Pokemon toys and did hip-hop dances. There was much talk about his "legacy," but it wasn't at all clear what that meant. The legacy of Harland Sanders was more complicated than an "original recipe" for fried chicken or the image of an old man in a white suit, albeit one so omnipresent as his. One thing everybody agreed on was that whatever else he was or represented, he was surely an icon in the truest sense of the word.

An icon, after all, doesn't mean a familiar face or symbol; Peter Frampton isn't an icon because he was hugely famous in the '70s. An icon, historically speaking, is an image that everyone can recognize, even if they can't read. Icons began as Byzantine religious figures and eventually became self-sufficient symbols that didn't require further explanation. That's why so many bars and restaurants have names like The Blue Parrot and The Spotted Pig—because they were originally named for the signs that hung over them. Later still, as applied semiotics became a cottage industry in the twentieth century, a number of imaginary persons were created who are still around today: Aunt Jemima and Uncle Ben (no relation), the Jolly Green Giant, Ronald McDonald, Mr. Clean, and the rest. Created from whole cloth and wholly malleable by their authors, these commercial "mascots" do their jobs well, soldiering along on behalf of their makers, decade after decade, until they are either retrofitted or summarily dismissed from service. But none of these has the universal weight, or power, of Colonel Sanders, for the simple reason that only Colonel Sanders, among the world's great global icons, was an actual person.

And he wasn't just an actual person; this was a complicated man who lived a very long, varied, and eventful life—a life that said much about three centuries in American history. Born in the rural hinterlands in what amounted to frontier conditions, coming into adulthood in the machine age, living long enough to appear in commercials shown during *Magnum, P.I.* breaks, he now exists as an image visible from space, a postmodern construct, a language all his own. Colonel Sanders was born

2

in the nineteenth century, in a place that might as well have been the eighteenth, lived deep into the twentieth century, and continues to be a larger-than-life presence in the twenty-first. He took a food that was especially resistant to commercialization on a big scale and made it as common as hamburgers—an astounding feat, given the long backstory and cultural freight of fried chicken and the physical difficulties of the dish itself. (Forget eleven herbs and spices; just making it well at all in a restaurant still is almost impossible for reasons I will explain later.)

The Colonel, as he was universally known, was not an accidental hero, a man who fell into a moment of history and was made immortal. No, through a mixture of ambition, showmanship, and dogged endurance, along with an intuitive grasp of what was then being called "mass culture," he found a way to make himself something bigger than just Harland Sanders and even bigger than a fast-food mogul. More than almost anyone in the hagiographic literature of American business, he truly lived the American Dream, as his friend and eulogist John Y. Brown Jr. rightly observed. His story paralleled the American Dream and in some way personified it. But what does the American Dream mean? Often it is used to describe hard work leading to fortune, but there is nothing especially American about that; that is the Protestant work ethic wrapped in a flag. The phrase "American Dream" was coined specifically to describe a state of egalitarian opportunity, a *novus orbis* where a man might transcend his roots and create himself as he saw fit. The historian James Truslow Adams, who is given credit for coining the phrase in his 1931 book *The Epic of America*, defined it thus:

> The American Dream is that dream of a land in which life
> should be better and richer and fuller for every man, with
> opportunity for each according to ability or achievement . . .
> It is not a dream of motor cars and high wages merely, but a
> dream of social order in which each man and each woman
> shall be able to attain to the fullest stature of which they

3

are innately capable, and be recognized by others for what they are, regardless of the fortuitous circumstances of birth or position.[2]

It was not, in other words, merely the chance to climb the social ladder; it was the chance to transcend who one was. Certainly, Harland Sanders came from a very low place on the social scale, although not as low as he might have; he was, after all, a white Protestant and a man, among other things. His belief in betterment as a moral calling was absolute and was underscored for him by his escape from rural poverty not once but several times. While he wasn't literally born in a log cabin, he might as well have been; late in the nineteenth century he came into the world of rural subsistence farming not much different from the one in which his pioneer forefathers lived. He embraced the gospel of business as ardently as any Babbitt and might have been portrayed as a buffoon by Sinclair Lewis or Sherwood Anderson. (To the end of his life he was an enthusiastic Rotarian, repeating the "Four Way Test" of good business and good morals.) His fortunes were made once with the rise of the railroad, once with the rise of the auto, and once again with the advent of corporate fast food and modern mass media, which took with one hand as they gave with the other. His posthumous history as the most prized asset of a great corporation tells the continuing story of that dream, too. After his death, his image was the soul of a vast global enterprise, torpid and somnolent in the '70s and then folded into the most infamously buccaneering corporations in the late '80s. In the 1990s it settled into the bosom of a vast and stable monopoly before spinning off again, this time as the vanguard of globalist expansion. Through a freak of history, Harland Sanders bridged the cultural history of three centuries of American striving; he personifies it in some special, unrepeatable way. There can never be another one like him.

1

"IT LOOKS LIKE
≡ YOU'LL NEVER AMOUNT ≡
TO ANYTHING"

arland Sanders, the oldest of three children, was born in 1890 to Wilbert and Margaret Ann Sanders of Henryville, Indiana, a farming community in the southernmost part of the state. They were not very poor by the standards of their time and place, a community of farmers laboring on hundred-acre plots for what amounted to basic sustenance. Wilbert Sanders died five years later, leaving two sons and one daughter in the care of his wife, a stout-hearted, fatalistic, devoutly religious woman in the unenviable position of being widowed, at thirty, with three young mouths to feed, in the rural Indiana of 1895. No one can fully appreciate the Colonel's life and character without understanding both how desperate and how unexceptional was his mother's situation. To be a relatively secure farmer in that time and place meant, at best, a level of desperation and privation that most Americans can barely imagine. The Panic of 1893, the worst depression the Unites States had yet faced, wrecked the nation's economy, and farmers, arguably, took it hardest: they were subject to ruinous usury by banks, outright theft at the hands of real estate speculators and railroads, and little hope of getting either credit or hard currency. But the Sanderses weren't even on that level; the family was struggling to survive on a basic subsistence level not far from life as it had been lived in frontier days—a period barely three generations removed. (Indiana was admitted as a state in 1816.)

Margaret Ann Sanders considered her position. She was a respectable Christian woman with a good reputation. She had eighty acres of productive land but couldn't farm them herself while raising three small children. She did own the property outright, so she could have "let it out," allowing somebody even poorer to work it in exchange for some portion of the proceeds, but it wasn't big enough to sharecrop. Her situation was tenuous. Still, farm communities like Henryville's were cohesive, and people tended to support each other since nobody else was going to, and so she was able to get by for a couple of years by sewing and doing housework for neighbors—an indignity she no doubt bore with the stoic patience of her Protestant forebears. In 1897, when Harland was seven, though, a steadier financial stream was needed, and so she went to work in a local canning factory. This is the first time in the Sanders story that the family's arc intersects with modern times; up until this moment, nothing had happened that would have been cause for comment during James Madison's administration. Nor, for that matter, would Margaret's solution of what to do with the kids surprise any poor, single mother struggling in the twenty-first century: she put her oldest in charge of his younger brother and sister and hoped for the best. The Colonel, for his part, loved telling the story about the first time he took over the kitchen, baking a loaf of bread in a hot wood stove and proudly presenting it to his mother at the canning factory. The other women on the line all hugged and kissed the boy, a story he would retell decades later as an old man being showered with the country's adoration.

The early life of Harland Sanders, though, was for the most part a depressing one. No one would want to make it into a TV movie. His mother sent him off to clear brush and scrubwood for a neighboring farmer—the kind of dull, relentless, lonely work that one tends to associate with chain gangs. He was ten.

His biographer John Ed Pearce, a *Louisville Courier-Journal* reporter, points out that "it was not particularly hard work" and says, as the Colonel did, that the main problem with the assignment was that Sanders goofed off instead of bending himself to his work. "There was no one to keep him to his task," Pearce writes, "and he took to spending a lot of time lying on his back looking and listening to the sounds of nature." Nature is not long in punishing such indolence, and the lesson came quickly when the ten-year-old was fired and told by the neighbor, "You're not worth a doggone, boy."[1]

The shame of his failure he seems to have carried with him for the rest of his life. He dreaded having to go back to his mother and tell her that he had failed both her and his helpless little brother and sister. Nor was his dread misplaced: "It looks like you'll never amount to anything," the Colonel remembered her saying. "I'm afraid you're just no good. Here I am, left alone with you three children to support, and you're my oldest boy, the only one that can help me, and you won't even work enough so somebody will keep you. I guess I'll never be able to count on you."[2]

The Colonel's second wife, Claudia Ledington (the one everybody remembers), said this speech had a formative effect on the boy, one that acted as a tonic, motivating him to his monumental exertions of later years. Like many children of single mothers, he utterly worshipped his mother's memory and cringed inwardly at the thought of not living up to her churchly piety and hard-work nostrums. Even in his eighties, as one of the most famous people in America, he never seemed to question his upbringing or the injunctions received at his mother's knee. He could, of course, never live up to them; though from his boyhood he had eschewed smoking, drinking, and gambling, he was afraid until the end of his days that his "cussing" would condemn him to eternal perdition. There were no mint juleps for the Colonel—only hard, unremitting self-flagellation, the very picture of the Protestant work ethic back when the Protestant work ethic really meant something.

A month after his dismissal he was back at work, this time as a coolie for one Henry Monk, who had a bigger farm in the southernmost part of the county. Sanders plowed the ground with a team of mules all day and then, though wobbly with fatigue, was expected to feed, water, and milk the cows, which inevitably kicked the boy, too. That was his life on Monk's farm the summer he was eleven: up before dawn, working until 10 p.m., getting his first calluses, and learning the value of hard work. In the approving words of John Ed Pearce, speaking for old-school Kentuckians everywhere, "Harland returned home with a new sense of dignity, and more money than he had ever had. But he had learned now what it was like to be on his own, to do a man's work, make a living. After that, school seemed childish and a waste of time."

It goes without saying that no modern biographer of the Colonel would take such a parental, approving tone—even if he or she felt it, which is equally unlikely. (The Colonel himself evidently felt keenly his lack of schooling and openly regretted it in later years when he struggled mightily to enter the middle class.) There was, in any case, no chance for him to get an education, given the still dire necessities of supporting his family. At the age of sixteen he was out working full time in the first of a long series of jobs that he would get, briefly excel at, and then either quit or be fired from. What all of these jobs have in common, however, is that they were urban, salaried positions a man of spirit could pick up and put down if they didn't suit him. There was to be no more farmwork for Sanders; he was now a twentieth-century man.

An uncle worked for the streetcar company in nearby New Albany, Indiana, so the young Harland Sanders got a job there in 1906 taking fares, making change, and exchanging his already developing line of patter with riders. But with tensions brewing in Cuba, there was a call for volunteers to head there, and Sanders joined the Army. It was both brief and dismal: his experience seems to have consisted entirely of shoveling mule feces and being seasick. He lost forty pounds from an already wiry frame. Landing in New Orleans, he caught a freight train up the Mississippi River and saw St. Louis for the first time. The feeling of riding the rails was addictive, and he gave himself over to it, traveling all around the South and eventually arriving in Sheffield, Alabama, where he had kin. Among these was an uncle who worked for the Southern Railway, and he got the seventeen-year-old Sanders a terrible job as a blacksmith's helper. This was a railroad job that wasn't anywhere near a train, a brutal job at best, made far worse, in the Colonel's recollection, because the blacksmith was a mean old hack who forced his underlings to hammer metal while it was still cold. It was, nevertheless, a railroad job, and it led to other railroad jobs, all of them equally menial but none as medieval as the first. The allure of the railroad, of course, was its modernity— the freedom, the way it collapsed distance, how it roared out of nowhere to disrupt the stasis and stultification of rural life in the nineteenth century. Colonel Sanders came from a time and place in which life was so boring that people actually stood around waiting for a train to pass. As a young man of spirit it was only natural that he would long to be a part of that world, even if it was only as a section hand driving spikes into the tracks or working the yards near stations or "firing" the engine by shoveling coal into its burning belly, which at least got him on the train, if briefly. It was a signal part of his character that he thrust himself into wherever the action was hottest; were he still alive, there can be no doubt he would be funding social media startups and investing in artisanal micro-distilleries.

It's also worth noting that the railroad era he was entering was very nearly at its end. The automobile was still a novelty, something one put on a body-length "duster" and goggles to drive. The first Model T was produced in 1908, and the culture it created would be the one that he tried, over and over again, to exploit from one or another angle. Such tireless, dynamic, amorphous energy wasn't just a response to the jazz age but the very spirit of it.

One of the oddities but also one of Sanders' special strengths was that while thriving in the rootless mobility of the age, he was very much a product of rooted, agrarian life. So in 1909 he married one of his first girlfriends, Josephine King, and promptly tied himself to the responsibility of raising a family with her before he had even begun to explore his newfound freedom. This is not a cynical view of his marriage; it was his own view, which was realistic and unsentimental. It seems never to have occurred to him to do otherwise. He met Josephine outside a movie theater, dated her for a few weeks, and decided to marry her. By his account, she turned out to be quiet, moody, and sexually unresponsive. It was a bad marriage all around, and the couple divorced after thirty-nine years.

Josephine bore three children but seems to have been little interested in lovemaking after that—an especially unfortunate circumstance given Sanders' passionate and hot-blooded nature. He found his pleasures elsewhere, as his second wife's nephew Don Ledington delicately but succinctly put it: "If [Josephine] wasn't interested in that part of his life, obviously, he didn't just forget about that part; he found what he needed to find in other places."[3]

The immediate effect of the marriage was to force Sanders to become a provider again. He found a fireman job on the Norfolk and Western shoveling coal into the engine. It was a great job as far as Sanders was concerned, except that it kept him away from his children and his wife, who, for some reason, wasn't answering his letters. Word got back that she had taken their babies and moved to her parents' home in Jasper, Alabama. When he got back home, he found not only that she had moved out but that she had given away all the furniture. This was a problem. "That hurt me," the Colonel remembered later. "I figured she didn't have any right to take my children and give away my furniture. But I didn't know anything to do about it."[4] Sanders set upon a plan to kidnap the children and went so far as to clamber about in his in-laws' bushes before he had a wise change of heart. According to the only account we have of the encounter, the Colonel's, Josephine agreed to take Sanders back with no more explanation than she gave for leaving him. He fell right back into the family man's responsibility, a joyless one he would bear for four decades. (If ever his mother's injunction to be responsible was put to the test, this was surely the time.)

And now Harland Sanders, the future Colonel, first raised his head from the menial jobs that had been his lot since childhood. Sanders got his first whiff of white-collar life when, in the aftermath of a train wreck, he realized that the first lawyer on the scene would be able to sue for damages on behalf of his clients, but only if he could get to the injured parties before they signed their rights away to a railroad claims adjuster for one dollar or more, "depending on how much blood was on them," as he would later remember. Sanders started working the dazed crowd with power-of-attorney forms using the hard-sell method that would later sway so many potential franchisees. Although the claims adjuster showed up soon afterward, Sanders was able to get enough clients to sign that he made $2,500 out of the accident—a small fortune for him and the first real money he ever made. This was the moment Sanders discovered his ability to shine under the spotlight, though this tendency had gone unnoticed during his days as a railroad drone or remarked upon by either his stoical mother or bride. (His second wife, Claudia, observed that "he was a natural showman. Any time he could get out front, promote something, get all the attention, that was him.")[5]

To Sanders' credit, it was an impulse that preceded even his own self-interest. Despite having only the scantest education, his new hero became Clarence Darrow, and he enrolled in a series of correspondence courses to become a lawyer. In 1915 in Arkansas, where he and his family were then living, pretty much anyone who "read the law" could represent a client in court—at least in the courts of justices of the peace where minor matters were settled—provided he could get a client. Since a half-educated lawyer was better than none at all, there was always a market. In small-town courts, personal connections and charisma went a long way. After the railroad accident claims were settled, there followed a very brief legal career, which might have been longer had not the impulsive Sanders decided, after a few promising months working the bar, to convince the Arkansas state legislature to limit the powers of the justice of the peace.

Even the Colonel, recollecting in tranquility many decades later, said he made a big hit at the hearings, but at a price: "I knocked myself out of a job." He alienated the very people with whom he was working in his new career. A short time later, he finished this chapter of his work life with an act considered beyond the pale even by the low professional standards of an Arkansas small-town court: he got into a fistfight with his own client while in court and directly in front of the judge. He was arrested and charged on the spot with battery, and not even his hero Darrow could have gotten Sanders out of that one.

That was the end of the Colonel's legal career, and his fall after that too-brief ascent was a steep one: he was back pounding steel rails as a section hand for the Pennsylvania Railroad at $1.65 a day—a wage he supplemented by unloading coal all night for $6 a shift. This was the reality that undergirded his entire existence, both then and for decades afterward: being an adult with a family to support, working the lowest menial trade. He wanted to be able to approach the higher strata of the society he lived in on equal terms. He understood that in the professional classes you weren't just selling your labor; you were selling yourself. And he was a natural salesman. He wanted to wear a white shirt himself, a white collar; and, though he never dreamed of it yet, the time would come when he would wear an entire white suit.

Much criticism would come, in mid-century, on this aspect of American business life. C. Wright Mills, in his widely read *White Collar*, put it in the starkest terms:

> In a society of employees dominated by the marketing mentality, it is inevitable that a personality market should arise.

> For in the great shift from manual skills to the art of "han-
> dling," selling and servicing people, personal or even intimate
> traits of employees are drawn into the sphere of exchange
> and become commodities in the labor market.[6]

That was perfectly fine with Sanders. In fact, it overjoyed him.
By the time of his apotheosis as Colonel Sanders he would have
utterly completed his transformation from worker to living
asset; his white suit would never be seen with a spot of dirt or
grease on it. Why would it? It would be his job to represent the
chicken, not to actually cook it. He himself, he came to understand, was a commodity, and while his background was dirt
poor, he was endowed with a million-dollar personality. He
meant to use it to claw his way back into the middle class he
had briefly glimpsed as a country lawyer.

He began this quest in earnest in 1921. Having heard that
there was a job available as an insurance salesman for Pru-
dential, he went out and bought himself a gray suit and a pair
of shiny black shoes and pitched himself with such energy and
conviction that the company took a chance on him. He was
given the worst territory in Indiana, occupied by the poorest residents and the most deadbeats. A man used to working
twenty backbreaking hours a day, he was not at all discour-
aged and went after commissions "like a possum after per-
simmons."[7] Through a combination of salesmanship, craft (he
would show up at a home and say he was taking a survey, one of
the questions of which was, "Do you have life insurance?"), and
sheer force of will, the thirty-one-year-old Sanders was able, in
a little more than a year, to head up his own district. But just
as with his career as a lawyer, his ungovernable truculence got
the best of him.

It was explained to him that he would be given his commission only after he turned in his accounts; the accounts, to
his mind, were his only means to get paid, and so he refused.
He was fired. Even though he desperately wanted to be in
the middle class, Sanders had no real idea of how the middle

class actually operated. "He wasn't a very good businessman," his partner John Y. Brown Jr. would later say. "He just didn't have the background to understand some parts of the business world."[8] Happily, this was at a time when, if you were turned out of one job, you could go to the next town and get one just like it. The elaborate machinery of the professional world, with its intersecting network of recommendations, credit reports, human resource departments, and all the rest was not yet even a bad dream. Sanders crossed the river into Louisville and got another job, this one with Mutual Benefit Life of New Jersey. He joined the Young Businessman's Club. He repeated numerous inspirational mottos. He redoubled his efforts to sell insurance as no man had sold insurance before. But it was obvious to him that he was not cut out to be a salary man. No sooner had he settled in Louisville than he decided to start a ferryboat company in order to replace *Old Asthma*, the ancient ferry by which the Charon of Kentucky took travelers across the river.

The ferryboat, named the *Froman M. Coots*, was, improbably, a success. Sanders passed it off as a lark in his memoir, saying, "Shucks, I didn't hang around . . . long enough to participate in the activities of the ferryboat company."[9] He didn't elaborate. But from this point forward, Harland Sanders was no longer a hardscrabble striver trying to cobble together a living; he was now an established small-town businessman, a Rotarian, a Roaring Twenties booster drumming up investments and welcoming working enterprise.

The Rotary Club, of course, is a service organization founded in 1905 by high-minded businessmen in Chicago and was one of the preeminent fraternal clubs of the twentieth century. Like-minded businessmen gloried in these organizations, which allowed a temporary respite from the tyranny of women, as they sometimes said, in addition to establishing matchless networking and deal-making opportunities. It was a friendless fellow indeed in the 1920s who was not in the Rotarians, Masons, Elks, Moose Lodge, or other such association. During the professionalization of small-town America in that period, these groups had a central importance in bringing together the middle-class consensus represented by President Calvin Coolidge.

The small-business pietism of the Rotarians hit Harland Sanders' sweet spot; he never saw any conflict between God and Mammon, between doing good and doing well. Like so many other optimistic entrepreneurs in America, he saw getting ahead as doing God's work, even if, as here, it took the form of a secular sacrament. Sanders was struck by the profundity of the Rotarians' slogans "He profits most who serves best" and "Service before self" ("That implied real service, don'cha see?"),[10] and later he would go on to recommend to everyone the Rotarian commandments known as the Four Way Test: "Is it the truth? Will it be fair to all concerned? Will it build goodwill and better friendships? Will it be beneficial to all concerned?" Sanders claimed for the rest of his life to have taken the Four Way Test seriously as an ultimate predictor of business success, which is a telling point, given that the Four Way Test is so high-minded and obviously misguided. It would be closer to the truth to say that no business transaction of any scale has ever passed even a single one of its absolute conditions. But, of course, it's the conflation of business and morality that most characterized the booster mentality. Today the 1920s booster is remembered largely from the scurrilous portraits etched in acid by urbane writers like H. L. Mencken, John Dos Passos, and Sinclair Lewis, who delighted in portraying the booster as a boob and a philistine, the very embodiment of stifling conformity.

Boosterism and the fraternal organizations that promoted it might be behind one of the most persistent myths that have survived the Colonel to this day. Starting in the 1970s, it was frequently asserted in private and later via the Internet that Colonel Sanders had been a secret member of the Ku Klux Klan and had willed part of his fortune to the "Invisible Empire." This urban legend carried so much power that a blaxploitation movie, *Darktown Strutters* (1975), bought into the myth, featuring as it does a Colonel clone, Commander Cross, who houses a Klan cell in his basement. Sanders' will is public, and therefore those allegations are easy enough to refute, but as there is no way to prove definitively that he wasn't in the Klan—the Klan being notably secretive about its membership—a quick look at the sources of this myth might be worthwhile. It should be said here, before going any further, that Harland Sanders seems to have been utterly without racial prejudice of any kind. No one who has spoken to me for this book nor any credible source in any of the primary or secondary literature about him has even hinted at bigotry or animosity on Sanders' part. Like all southerners of his time, he said "Negro" until informed by some well-meaning person that the term had become offensive. (It did not become so until the mid-1960s; Martin Luther King used it in his "I Have a Dream" speech in 1963.) In fact, the head of public relations for Kentucky Fried Chicken in the early 1970s was a black man named Ray Calander. Having spent a significant amount of time shuttling around with the Colonel during those years, Calander claims to be the one to have told him that he preferred to be called "black." The Colonel replied, "Well, I wouldn't call you nice folks black."[11]

That said, it does not appear implausible that the Klan, in the form it took in the 1920s—a fraternal organization dedicated to networking and drinking as much as to the eradication of Catholics, Jews, and Negroes—would be an unthinkable fit for a young, ambitious Harland Sanders. Had he joined, it would have been entirely for business purposes; he never displayed any interest in politics at any time in his long life other than making ceremonial appearances at parades and a brief, equally ceremonial stint as "regional director" of the Kentucky Chamber of Commerce in the 1950s. The so-called Second Klan, which reached its peak in the 1920s and claimed five to six million members (with a disproportionate number of the South's rising young businessmen), was demographically not very different from some of the other Babbittesque fraternal organizations of the time, such as the Rotary Club, Elks,

Masons, and so on. The young Sanders, eager to better himself
in the world and an inveterate joiner, might have signed on for
some short time. If so, he never spoke of it, and there is not the
slightest hint of evidence for his having done so. It seems far
more likely that as the nation's most conspicuous elderly white
southerner, Harland Sanders was a slate upon which dark sus-
picions could be written.

A man with a family to support, grappling for a toehold in
the middle class and all its totems represented a form of salvation to Harland Sanders. The society into which he was born
was one in which the classes were far more amorphous and
permeable than they might have been fifty years earlier or fifty
years later. Just as the lack of a high school diploma hadn't
stopped him from becoming a lawyer, his brief and piecemeal
experience as a twice-fired insurance salesman didn't prevent
Sanders from taking a job as secretary of the Chamber of Commerce of Columbus, Indiana. He stayed on the job for an unre-
warding year, finding it impossible to promote business and
Rotarian goodwill in a small city dominated by large manufac-
turing interests. He quit that job, too, and, thinking of the success of his riverboat venture, sank his remaining money into a
scheme to manufacture acetylene lamps. He would sell these
to farmers to replace the weak, dangerous kerosene lamps then
common. Again, this was a project that no businessman in his
right mind would ever have conceived, since farmers had no
money to begin with. Harland Sanders, of all people, should
have known, as the scion of a poor farm family, that farmers
of the sort he was looking to sell to in southern Indiana either
didn't have money to spend on trifles or, if they did, would fall
behind in payments with almost geological predictability. To
make matters worse, at almost the exact time Sanders started
the business, Delco introduced a small electric generator that
would power lights for farms outside the reach of county power
lines. The acetylene lamp factory went down in flames, so to
speak, and Harland Sanders was, once again, wiped out.

Sanders cast around for his next move. The idea of moving

to a bigger city seems not to have occurred to him; but by the early '20s, modernity had come to Indiana in the form of the automobile, and word had gotten around that the Michelin tire company needed a salesman. Like many Americans of his generation, Sanders had come of age with the railroad. It had been his first job, his first liberation, his first means of escape from the grinding, immemorial tedium of subsistence farming. To the end of his life he remained enchanted by the romance of trains, their noise and rhythmic, clacking power. But the railroad era was over, and with the coming of the auto a new sector was opening up—one that a man of spirit could utilize. A natural salesman, Sanders could as easily have sold cars as tires, but tires were what came his way. The job he talked himself into was something of a plum, with a $750 guaranteed salary each month if he met his quota. Given that he had the entire state of Kentucky as his territory and his ever-enlarging acquaintance with various businessmen around the state—to say nothing of his ready line of patter, still Sanders' greatest asset—he immediately made a success of his new job. There was nothing he would not do in the service of the company, and his first position of living icon was his role as Bibendum, the company mascot made of tires. Sanders would don his Michelin Man suit and go around to fairs and public events boasting of the product's advantages and putting its local rivals to the test, often in the form of having muscular farm boys inflate the tires to see which popped first. Like everything else in the Colonel's life until Kentucky Fried Chicken came along, this career followed the usual trajectory: he quickly became the top tire salesman in Kentucky, but then in 1924, for reasons that remain murky, he either left the company or was fired and found himself back at square one.

A horrible auto accident had totaled both cars, in addition to splitting his head open (a wound the resilient Sanders treated by pushing the skin flaps together on his scalp, or so he claimed many years later). But the upshot was that in this new age of motoring he was reduced to hitchhiking. He lucked into a fate-

18

ful ride with a representative of Standard Oil whom he was able to talk into letting him take over a gas station in Nicholasville. His usual combination of hustle, palaver, and hard work paid off. The station was a success, and Sanders was able to move his family to town. In 1928 he was even able to send his oldest daughter, Margaret, to college. Two years later the station closed but not due to Sanders' unmellowed temper or the frequent brawls he got into; the Depression was reason enough for the Standard Oil company to close the Nicholasville station. But soon another one became available in Kentucky, and executives at the Shell oil company, having heard of his success in Nicholasville, gave him a marginal station in Corbin, Kentucky, to run rent free. It was thought that if he could make a go of it the place wouldn't be a total loss, and he could pay the company a penny a gallon extra in lieu of rent. That penny ended up going a long way.

The location was on a busy road, Highway 25, where it faced a larger, more visible station across the road. But the bigger challenge was the area's rough trade notoriety. A locus of bootlegging, its northern corner was called Hell's Half-Acre by locals, owing to the infamous frequency of fights and even gun battles there. (During his time in Corbin, Sanders kept a gun under the cash drawer and a shotgun he called his "hawg rifle" next to his bed at home.) The city was a violent one; during the "red summer" of 1919, a decade earlier, the city expelled all its black citizens in what amounted to a race riot and adopted what southern blacks call a "Don't let the sun go down on you" attitude.[12]

This was the city where Sanders launched his new career. It took a tough man to set up business in Corbin. There was no local Rotary chapter to join. Nobody cared about the Four Way Test. But Harland Sanders pushed and promoted the store with his usual passion, even in the face of threats by his direct competitor, a man named Matt Stewart, who had opened a Standard Oil station down the road a short time earlier. The two men had strong wills, hot tempers, and itchy fists. It was only a matter of time before the feud came to a head. Sanders painted a big sign on a railroad wall near the highway directing drivers his way. Stewart responded by painting the sign over. Sanders paid a little call on Stewart and offered to "blow [his] goddamn head off."[13] Sanders went ahead and repainted the sign. The response was predictable, but the timing was bad. He was conferring with two Shell officials, district manager Robert Gibson and a supervisor, H. D. Shelburne, when word came that Stewart was painting it over again. The three men, all armed to the teeth, jumped into a car and headed down to the sign. Stewart was on a ladder painting it over and, seeing the men, jumped down and pulled his weapon. Bullets flew, and the Shell manager was killed instantly with three bullets to the heart. Sanders jumped into the breach and under withering fire grabbed his fallen comrade's gun. He and Shelburne flanked Stewart, who was hidden behind a wall. The future Colonel unloaded with true aim and hurled hot lead into Stewart's shoulder, even as Shelburne unloaded into the Standard Oil man's hip.

"Don't shoot, Sanders!" Stewart cried. "You've killed me." As it happened, he hadn't.

The police arrested everyone, and the case went to court. It may have been the simple findings, the power of Shell, or the Colonel's way with words, but when all was said and done, Sanders and Shelburne had their charges dismissed, and Stewart was given eighteen years for murder. Two years later, Stewart was still appealing his conviction when he was shot and killed by a deputy sheriff who, it was rumored, had been paid by the family of the slain Robert Gibson. Pearce mentions the rumor in Sanders' biography but adds, suggestively, that "the charges were never proved."[14]

Having won the right to sell gas in Corbin by feat of arms, Harland Sanders made a great success of his station. His lifelong enterprise, hustle, and gregariousness more or less guaranteed that his gas station would be a success. His was the first station in the area to offer oil checks, free air pumping, and other services still novel in rural Kentucky. The drivers who came through frequently asked Sanders where they could get something to eat. There wasn't much in the area. Now, Sanders fed his family in the station every day. Sometimes he even invited travelers to come in and join them. So it occurred to him: why not make a little something on the side? There was a small room on the side of the station, so Sanders bought some linoleum on credit for sixteen dollars and moved the family dining room into it. They had food ready at 11 a.m., since easterners were used to eating at noon, and if none of them showed up, the family could eat the midday meal. If somebody did show up, the family would cook more later. Sanders made all his southern favorites, such as ham, biscuits, greens, and, of course, fried chicken, cooked in a big skillet like all good southern cooks. This was the first form ancestor of all modern Kentucky Fried Chicken. Rather than an afterthought to a full tank of gas, the food soon became a major sideline—so much so that the Colonel, never one to miss a chance for promotion, changed the name of his business from Sanders Service Station to Sanders Service Station and Cafe and then, as the food business continued to expand, to Sanders Cafe and Service Station. When a four-room transient shack next door became available, Sanders took it over and made it into a motel-restaurant, Sanders Court and Cafe.

The names changed, but the character of the place did not. It was a gas station with some rooms attached, in a backward corner of a backward state, in the grip of the Depression, and it was a desperate undertaking, like most small businesses were at that place and time. A family with hungry children had to be fed, clothed, and housed from the proceeds of a gas station at a time when gas was a few cents a gallon. Selling food to travelers was just a way to get more people in to buy gas so the family could make a few dollars more than they might have previously. The food wasn't a major source of profit; the Sanders family had to buy food, and if no travelers came, they would eat it themselves, the way all marginal, isolated restaurant owners do. Such cash as was kept in the register was essentially the family bank, and if anyone needed some they would take it out and leave a note in its place saying how much they took and when.[15] But by 1935 the motel was doing so well that two other motels nearby existed off its spillover business, according to the Colonel's daughter Margaret.

Nothing represented the communal nature of rural poverty more than fried chicken. Not everybody has hogs and a smokehouse, and it goes without saying that the poorest Kentuckians were not the sort of people who had herds of cattle contentedly grazing on broad, green fields. No, the rural poor, in Kentucky and throughout the South and for that matter the world, were lucky to have a few yardbirds scratching around, eating bugs and dirt, and laying an occasional precious egg. On Sundays and other special occasions, that kind of family might kill a chicken and cut it up so everyone could have a piece. They would fry it up in lard and season it with spices as they had been taught to do by West African slaves who brought the trick with them from their lost homes. Fried chicken wasn't a snack treat but a staple, and far from a symbol of heaping bounty as it was later to become commercially, it was rather a fall-back, the homiest and humblest of Sunday meals. It was therefore the preeminent food for poor people in the South, and when they served it to strangers they shared a part of their family life. In that much, the marketing message trumpeted by the chain many years later was not entirely without foundation. Fried chicken, to the Colonel's mind, was not really something that you ate in restaurants. It was a part of home life. Many southerners understood this and continue to understand it in a way the rest of the world does not. Colonel Sanders, though not exactly a southerner himself, was southern enough, and more than southern enough to embody fried chicken.

For one thing, he understood that simply taking chicken parts, dredging them in flour, and dropping them into boiling oil alongside french fries and onion rings wasn't really fried chicken. Fried chicken is very difficult to make well and impossible in a fry basket; nearly every traditional recipe, going back to the very first published cookbook in America, *The Virginia*

House-Wife's Cookbook (1824), calls for cooking it in a heavy pan. Heavy pans full of lard or oil are unwieldy and messy and difficult to handle. They also take a long time to cook food. Most of all, they require great skill on the part of the cook, which is one reason making great fried chicken was a special badge of honor among southern matriarchs, white and black.

Without really knowing it, Sanders attempted to mass-produce this venerated dish, essentially the national food of the American South, for the first time. He did it blindly at first, ad hoc, and without any business plan to speak of. Later, he got help from seasoned restaurateurs and bankers and corporate entrepreneurs. But only a figure like Sanders could have bridged the private and public life of fried chicken, just as only he could have projected the image of a white-suited "southern gentleman" with perfect relevance alongside *The Mod Squad*.

All of this speaks to the cultural capital that Colonel Sanders brought to the business for which he is known today, Kentucky Fried Chicken. It also speaks to the paradox that he embodied. Anyone who knew anything of the South knew that no Kentucky colonel would have cooked the fried chicken in a southern household; the chicken in prosperous southern households, particularly in the Colonel's era, was inevitably cooked by a black maid or family housekeeper. Colonel Sanders created an alternative reality in which the white planter not only ate the chicken but implicitly made it. Nothing could have been further from the truth.

Likewise, he appeared to customers in mid-century to be an emblem of old-fashioned values, not in the abstracted commercial iconography of Gibson Girls and watch-fobbed men but in a historically appreciable, specific way. Yes, on some level the success of the business was based on a very good type of fried chicken. But that fried chicken was understood, rightly, as an expression of somebody who knew about fried chicken and the southern food culture that alone was capable of producing it at its best. In some indistinct but real way, Colonel Sanders was the personification of his own past—as a transplanted southerner, as a cook, as an old-fashioned, larger-than-life salesman, as the real deal. And part of his power was that people understood him as a man caught between eras. When he produced this most traditional of foods in a conspicuously ultramodern, space-age, high-tech restaurant that looked like nothing else on earth, the paradox was even plainer.

All this remained in the future. In the mid-1930s he was a well-respected motel owner. Ever the booster, he had made himself president of the Kentucky Restaurant Association. Though still uncommissioned, unbearded, and given to wearing only neat working clothes rather than a spotless white suit, he was by both nature and conscious decision the kind of larger-than-life personality that inevitably sticks in the minds of travelers. Also, his mania for cleanliness and good service, absorbed in the sternest of terms at his mother's knee, was in stark contrast to rural menus and diners of that time. The amenities offered in the rural motel, such as a no-tipping policy, complimentary umbrellas and car tarps during inclement weather, and even free newspapers, absolutely awed visitors. But it was the food that earned Sanders his first fame. It must have been a glorious day indeed when, after all those years of Sanders' politicking with local Rotarians, Governor Ruby Laffoon appeared in a black limousine with a full police escort to check the place out. Even the travel writer Duncan Hines, not yet elevated to his own cake-baking immortality, included Sanders Cafe in his 1935 *Adventures in Good Eating*, the nation's first road-food guide. In reality, the review is hardly a rave. Sanders Cafe, according to Hines, was "a very good place to stop en route to Cumberland Falls and the Great Smokies," notable for its "sizzling steaks, fried chicken, country ham, [and] hot biscuits."[16] The fried chicken is only mentioned in passing! But the fame of his restaurant had spread beyond Corbin—and even Kentucky—and this, too, was a first for its owner. In early middle age, it appeared that he had found his place in the world at last. But his story had not yet really begun.

2

≡ THE COMING OF THE COLONEL ≡

The suit was originally black. It came with a string tie and was distinctive enough in its way, but something about it lacked oomph, panache. The Colonel, it is reckoned by his contemporaries, began wearing it around 1950, about the time of his second and final commission. The first, given him by Governor Ruby Laffoon, was a ceremonial decree that pleased Sanders briefly but was by no means defining. He even lost the certificate over the years, leading to his being granted a second one in 1949 by Lieutenant Governor Lawrence Weatherby. He grew a moustache and goatee and let the hair on his head grow out. He made a string tie out of grosgrain ribbon and started introducing himself as Colonel Harland Sanders, and his associates went along with it, jokingly at first and then in earnest. "We used to ask him when he was going to change the name of his place to Colonel Sanders Court, sell Colonel Sanders Fried Chicken. Finally, I think everybody sort of accepted it," a Corbin friend told Sanders' biographer.[1] The rechristened Colonel Sanders even went so far as to have his beard bleached, as he was not yet old enough to have a white beard. He knew, though, that a paternal-looking southern gentleman was expected to have a white beard, and eventually he figured out that he would need a white suit, too. That came later, when

Harland Sanders, selling himself as Colonel Sanders and seeking to create a brand on the strength of his Corbin restaurant, had begun his Sisyphean labors of driving around the country trying to make it happen. He was sixty-five years old. He should have been enjoying his retirement. But it hadn't worked out that way.

The Corbin restaurant had been an unqualified success. On the strength of the Sanders Cafe's reputation—which now, thanks to Duncan Hines, extended from coast to coast—Sanders by 1945 had what seemed like the success of which he had always dreamed. He was making money hand over fist from the cafe, which had by 1937 expanded to 142 seats from its original 6—so much so that he had opened another motel in Richmond, Kentucky, and even one in Asheville, North Carolina, the home of the Biltmore mansion. Contemporaries suggest that its far distance from Josephine may have been one reason for such a sequel; there certainly wasn't much else to recommend it, and it soon closed. He opened a furniture store; he added rooms to the motel. He bought a plumbing supply store. He drove around in his white Cadillac and checked out a lot of restaurants, learning more about how the business was working, both regionally and nationally. When the cafe burned down in 1939, he is said to have received the news calmly and rebuilt it despite having had only $5,000 of fire insurance coverage. The new place did even better than the old one. He was, in short, a success. But there was a terrible shadow to his prosperity.

Harland Sanders had no son to pass on his business to; his son, Harland Jr., died at age twenty in 1932 of blood poisoning from a streptococcus germ picked up in the hospital, in one of those random tragedies so common in the years before the advent of antibiotics. Years later, when ruing his decision to sell Kentucky Fried Chicken, the senior Sanders would point to the absence of a male heir as one of the main reasons for that choice.[2] In reality, of course, the Colonel could no more have run Kentucky Fried Chicken than he could have piloted the space shuttle; even when there were only a handful of restaurants paying him a franchise fee for the use of his recipe and seasonings, the enterprise was already getting beyond what he could reasonably handle.

He had enough money to live comfortably and to provide for his family; he was well liked and respected in his community and even had something in the way of fame to show for his half-century of struggle. Things went along like that for a good long time and might easily have gone on that way until he died at the age of ninety. Had he been an ordinary restaurant owner, that would have been the story of Harland Sanders. His obituary in the local paper would have remembered him as a pillar of the community, a beloved family man, and a colorful character. It should have ended, "He is survived by his wife, Josephine, and his daughters Margaret and Mildred." But that is not what happened. Just when he was beginning to reap the rewards of a grueling life, disaster struck yet again, landing him penniless and jobless at the age of sixty-five. The state had been talking about linking U.S. 25, the road on which Sanders Cafe was positioned, with a new interstate mandated by the National Highway Act. Sanders thought the new traffic would put him over the top at last, pumping rich arterial blood into his business and poising him for long-awaited expansion. Then the news came down: U.S. 25 would be linked to the interstate, all right, but only after it was rerouted—away from Sanders Cafe. The business that he had built through unrelenting labor over twenty years became a dead issue more or less overnight. Sanders had lobbied ceaselessly to get the interchange put in place; but someone else lobbied more ceaselessly, or in any case more effectively, to get U.S. 25 moved elsewhere. Now Sanders' business was off the main road, a Bates Motel, and that was the end of the story. No amount of umbrella service or country ham could make a difference; larger forces were at play, and not even all of Sanders' legendary energy could sway them the tiniest bit. In this way, small-business owners are so very vulnerable; all it takes is one disgruntled customer, one bad review, one fire, and all can be lost.

Harland Sanders, still just a mortal man, had no power beyond his immediate surroundings. But what if he could be in more places than one? The fact that Sanders Court had been marooned on a local road was its death knell, but the Colonel had already been thinking of bigger things, ways to be bigger than just the guy with the best motel in southern Kentucky, for several years. The key was franchising. Franchising would allow Harland Sanders to be everywhere at once; to share his success with others, in the true Rotarian way; to be more places and to make more money than he ever had before.

The idea of franchising was an old one even in the mid-1950s. Essentially, it was an arrangement by which small businesses could build off of bigger, more successful ones. A small, independent business (say, a hamburger restaurant or car lot) paid to be part of a larger system with its own respected brand, like McDonald's or Ford. In return, the franchisees got a ready-to-sell product and various kinds of infrastructure support, such as special equipment, national advertising, and even a ready-to-go operations system like the legendary McDonald's operations "bible." The franchise was and is much more than just a business arrangement, though. It is America in microcosm, a federation of small, independent owners all in league with each other and with a central, defining institution. It's a profound invention, the very heart of the American Dream. At least in the early stages, it takes very little to purchase a franchise; frequently good character and a decent credit rating are all that is required to participate in a business far larger, more complex, and more rewarding than any citizen could plausibly expect to create on his or her own.

Kentucky Fried Chicken operates on essentially the same principle as all modern franchising relationships. An investor applies to the parent corporation, Kentucky Fried Chicken, for the right to own and operate a business site with that name. The franchise fee isn't usually that high; it was $20,000 in the 1960s and stayed in the $20,000–$30,000 range throughout the 1980s. The real hurdle isn't the franchise fee or the 9 percent commission on profits; that's money the franchisees never see and helps pay for national advertising, new product development, and other investments that company officials hope will be good for business. There are the costs of actually building the restaurant, which can range from $1 million to $2 million. But assuming that a potential franchisee has good credit, that kind of money can be borrowed from the bank. The one big block that today keeps many small-business owners from joining the Great Kentucky Soviet is the requirement that the applicant show a net worth of $1 million and at least $360,000 in liquid assets. Only millionaires need apply! Additionally, the current corporate owner of Kentucky Fried Chicken, a spin-off from PepsiCo called Yum! Brands, also insists that the franchisee take on the corporation's other properties, Taco Bell and Pizza Hut, and commit to opening multiple stores over a period of three to five years.

The difference between the average Kentucky Fried Chicken owner in the 1960s and one in our own time is, then, the very difference between Colonel Sanders and the senior management team at PepsiCo and Yum! Brands. What made all the fast-food businesses grow so fast was the accessibility to the mainstream it gave them. A restaurant might offer a good hamburger or great fried chicken thanks to the specially seasoned flour a flamboyant character called Colonel Sanders sold; through the mighty power of franchising, thousands could all not just sell special fried chicken but actually *be* a Kentucky Fried Chicken restaurant, exactly like all the others. The excellence of one not only guaranteed the excellence of the others and the concomitant success; it actually improved them. By aligning with something larger than themselves, the restaurants were better than any single one could ever be: more reliable, less prone to failure, labor crises, and so on.

Consider the note of triumphalism that comes from the first of all the great American fast-food chains, White Castle. "When you sit in a White Castle," a 1932 brochure told potential operators, remember that you are one of several thousands; you are sitting on the same kind of stool; you are being served on the same kind of counter; the coffee you drink is made in accordance with a certain formula; the hamburger you eat is prepared in exactly the same way over a gas flame of the same intensity; the cups you drink from are identical with thousands of cups that thousands of other people are using at the same moment; the same standard of cleanliness protects your food. . . . Even the men who serve you are guided by standards of precision which have been thought out from beginning to end.[3]

Of course, that kind of power, the result of thousands of identical businesses all drawing on the energy and dedication of small entrepreneurs, was not yet available to the Colonel. It was not even something he would have imagined. But the root of it was an arrangement, in the starkest and most intimate terms, between Colonel Sanders and a far-flung network of diners, roadhouses, and greasy spoons. It was as simple as this: they could serve a dish called Colonel Sanders' Kentucky Fried Chicken in exchange for a nickel for each chicken they sold, and they had to buy the equipment and special recipe (a pressure cooker and the seasoned flour) from Colonel Sanders himself. It was strictly a handshake deal, and the honor system was good enough for the Colonel. As for how they cooked "his" chicken and whether it might be up to his standards, that was a matter to be left to the Fates. He had neither the means nor, to be frank, the motivation to do so. He had his hands full making sure the flour was seasoned right with what would soon be known as his "eleven secret herbs and spices," and Claudia had enough help filling the bags up and mailing them out. It was up to the franchisees to make the chicken well. If they didn't, it wouldn't sell, and the Colonel would be left to live on his Social Security check.

The franchisees are the real heroes of Kentucky Fried Chicken. The story of Kentucky Fried Chicken starts with one man and continues with a series of impersonal corporate overlords. But its primary life force consists neither in buckets of fried chicken nor in the image of its iconic founder; it has grown and prospered and expanded, even in the shadow of the Great Wall of China, because of the franchisees who together forge into the future, bound by one business and by the endless, dispiriting struggle to run it well. There were no trips to Russia or Rose Bowl Parade rides for the franchisees; all they could hope for was to make a living. By working together as a great fried-chicken collective under the Colonel's banner, they were able to make a good income and put their kids through college. Harland Sanders was their Lenin, and the empire he built outlived communism, the Automat, and the betting odds. But first, he needed to truly re-create himself as the Colonel.

The physical part was easy enough, but what about the actual title? The twenty-first-century title has essentially no meaning to its public; as with General Tso or Sergeant Pepper, the rank is a vague honorific carried by a semifictional figure. Earlier in the chain's history, of course, it meant something; it was meant to broadcast to diners in faraway lands that this was a product of the Old South. The Kentucky colonelcy established in 1813, though predating even the cotton kingdom and its feudal plantation system, was dear to the hearts of post-Reconstruction boomers. It spoke to the magnolia-scented mythos of the Old South, the "lost cause," and its aristocratic gallantries. The position was always an honorary one that carried with it neither rank nor responsibility; the military music of its name was merely a theatrical effect, like epaulets or the ceremonial swords carried by Asian diplomats. Even by the trifling standards of such titles, the commission was easy to get, a political trifle given out by the governor with no restrictions whatsoever. According to the order's mission statement,

> The Honorable Order of Kentucky Colonels does not appoint or commission Kentucky Colonels. That can only be done by the sitting Governor of the Commonwealth. Only the Gover-

nor knows the reason for bestowing the honor of a Colonel's Commission on any particular individual.

This is an ideal qualification for a political honor—almost platonic. There are some hard and fast requirements, however:

> To obtain a Kentucky Colonel Commission, an applicant must be recommended by an individual who holds a Colonel Commission. The applicant must also be 18 years old. Further information can be obtained by contacting the Governor's Office in Frankfort. The address is Attention: Lora Quire, Room 8, Governor's Office, State Capital, Frankfort, KY 40601.

The colonelcy was indubitably a stroke of marketing genius—a guaranteed lock on the mythos of the Deep South and a whiff of magnolia for those faraway territories where Kentucky Fried Chicken had no natural constituency. The vaguely martial honor seems so antique and theatrical that it borders on the exotic; to somebody who never heard of a Kentucky Colonel, it's as gratifying and mysterious as the grandiose sobriquets created for themselves by African dictators.

The early 1950s were good years for Sanders. He had found at last the outlet for the larger-than-life persona that his personality seemed to demand and which had served fruitlessly in his various forays as businessman and booster. His new colonelcy served him well when things were going well; it certainly made him more memorable. But he still looked the same, albeit with a beard. When the bad news about the new highway came down from Lexington in 1955, he found himself with little else but his title, some affected facial hair, and a really great recipe for fried chicken. He was now sixty-five years old, broke, and with nothing to show for nearly twenty years of effort. The only mercy extended him was that he and Josephine had divorced in 1947, and he had married Claudia Ledington, a waitress at the cafe, in 1949. The two were inseparable. Claudia's steadfast loyalty was to be a great comfort to him at this dark hour. She was willing to do anything the Colonel asked—she managed to overcome her deeply ingrained shyness and reserve so she could walk around in antebellum dress in the last years of Sanders Cafe. She took his storms and rages in stride and as much as anyone helped make his business success a reality. He never needed her more than at that moment when all seemed lost. "The Colonel might say he didn't know what to do, but we who knew and understood him knew that it wouldn't be long before he would know exactly what to do," she later said. And so he did. "Claudia," he told his wife, "now that I have nothing pushing me I am going to put my efforts on my fried chicken. . . . I am going to improve it and introduce it to the public in other restaurants. In other words, I am going to franchise it."[4]

And now at sixty-five the Colonel was set to begin the most arduous job of his life and the one that would cement his fame. He wasn't looking for his first franchisee; three years earlier, a restaurant owner in Salt Lake City named Leon "Pete" Harman had put the Colonel's chicken on the menu, and a smattering of other places had accepted his nickel-a-chicken handshake offer. But that was when he was dealing from a position of strength. He had been a respected restaurateur, the keeper of a southern kitchen that had received national praise. He made a plenty of money and didn't really need those franchise fees. Now he did. It was a consummate act of salesmanship and self-promotion: he presented himself as a man with a product so famous and valuable that it alone could change the fortunes of failing restaurants. What's more, he projected all the warmth and friendship that would turn a potential franchiser into a member of his chicken "family"—even inviting each one, then and for many years after, to stay at his home and enjoy a breakfast cooked by the Colonel himself. This was an important bit of business—they might well have seen him as a needy, possibly even pathetic figure, an old drummer still on the road when he should be enjoying the fruits of his life's work.

The Colonel wasn't selling "fast food" then or afterward. His chicken, even in the pressure cooker, took a long time to make, and today the time cycle still hasn't shortened that much. The small restaurants to which he was able to sell his chicken were themselves homey affairs of the very kind that fast-food restaurants of the 1960s and '70s constantly referenced. The idea of a dedicated chicken restaurant was something that never occurred to him.

The physical demands of being on the road would have been wearisome even to a younger man. The Colonel and Claudia loaded up the car with bags of seasoned flour, the pressure cooker (more on this later), and some paper goods with the Colonel's likeness and the words "Kentucky Fried Chicken" printed on them. Then he hit the road, driving all day in Indiana and Illinois, looking for prospects. On some nights he slept in the backseat of his Cadillac in his white suit, shaving and combing his hair in the morning in a service station—no doubt inferior in every way to the one he had owned and run for twenty years in Corbin. He was an old man whose body had seen a lot of hard labor, and he had arthritis. He popped aspirins throughout the day. Frequently, he was dismissed or derided by people he visited. Kentucky Fried Chicken was built on the efforts of one old man tirelessly driving around to backroad diners nearly as decrepit as himself.

Dave Thomas, the founder of Wendy's, remembers meeting the Colonel during this era:

I had never seen a black suit like that in my life. [The Colonel's "white suit" period started later.] The coat had long tails and fit him perfectly. His graying goatee was perfectly trimmed and he carried a gold-tipped cane. Colonel Sanders was one of a kind . . . he introduced himself and asked if I knew him. I pretended I didn't even though I knew all about him. We sat down over a cup of coffee, and he talked to me like an old friend. I've never met a better salesman. When he left, I had a sense this man was going to change my life. . . . Maybe this Colonel in a white Cadillac had something.

After all, Thomas reasoned, "food is a personal thing, and it's tied closely to family life. People want to know the values of the person who is ladling out the goods. Harland Sanders stood for values that people understood and liked."[5] Many years later Thomas would take a page out of the Colonel's book and become the living personification of Wendy's—albeit without any of his mentor's flamboyance.

The Colonel well knew how to leverage his persona, taking great pains to emphasize his down-home origins and playing up his country lingo, dropping extra "dad gumbits" and "Don't ya sees?" in his conversations. It wasn't a sham; the Colonel's backcountry bona fides were unimpeachable. Still, there was a level of artifice. When he dictated business letters or talked business, there was nothing folksy about him. But in the mid-1950s, one of his favorite promotional tacks was to find a local radio or TV station and present himself as a guest on a talk show, bringing chicken with him and sometimes handing out drumsticks to the audience.

When a restaurant did adopt Kentucky Fried Chicken, the Colonel would make a public appearance, sometimes even bringing along Claudia in a full-dress antebellum ensemble and introducing her as "the Colonel's lady." On these memorable occasions, he would cook the chicken himself in the back. "Then," he would remember later, "when I got a supply of orders ahead, I'd go out and do what I called a 'a little colonel-ing.' I'd take off my apron, dust the flour off my pants, put on my vest, long-tailed coat, and gold watch chain, and go out into the dining room and talk to the guests."[6]

Neither the long-tailed coat nor the gold watch made it to the final uniform; the Colonel sometimes donned a black suit, as Kentucky colonels are wont to do, until he figured out that a white one was more immediately identifiable. It was television producers who told him how the white suit made him stand out, giving him a visual signature—an endowment that can hardly be overstated in the fast-food business, where image is everything.

Perhaps this is overstating matters. Image isn't everything. The most Herculean marketing efforts will be in vain if the product is inedible, the stores dirty, or the service insolent. But the enormous pressure of low costs and high volume tends to flatten out food quality in the quick-service restaurant business, or QSR, as it is known in the trade. And given that the market is continually saturated, all that separates one chain from another is its brand, which is to say its iconography.

That said, it would have been much easier for the Colonel if, like his handlers later in life, all he had to worry about was the use and misuse of his image. The problem was that especially in the early going, Sanders was concerned with matters beyond just marketing and public relations. As he saw it, the essence of his business, the thing that would make him rich again and so redeem his life, was the singular quality of his chicken. He had, he believed, found a way to re-create the tenderness and delicacy of traditional southern pan-fried chicken with something close to the ease and speed of open deep-frying. And this technology was the means by which he finally, after a lifetime of effort, found a product worthy of his salesmanship. The Colonel's image was all-important, and the innovations made by Pete Harman, his first and greatest franchisee, were of enormous importance to Kentucky Fried Chicken. But at the heart of it was the chicken itself, and what made the chicken great was the innovation of using a pressure cooker to make it. It's much less glamorous than any secret mixture of herbs and spices but far more important.

The pressure cooker, then a space-age novelty still on the cutting edge of gastronomy, was, in more ways than can be calculated, the perfect instrument and symbol of everything the Colonel was trying to do. For one thing, although it is sometimes associated in the minds of baby-boom historians with the 1950s culture of domesticity and plenty (the happy wife imagined in her kitchen filled with useless gadgets), in reality, like the Colonel himself, the appliance was a product of scarcity. Although the technology had been around in one form or another since the seventeenth century, pressure cooking never really hit it big in the United States until the Depression and then the war effort made home canning an economic necessity. There, in the stark and shabby kitchens of a million working-class homes, the machine was put to use making apple preserves or softening lentils. Like fried chicken, it was primarily a home technology as well. Fried chicken was the specialty of matriarchs wielding heavy pans who assembled their clans weekly for ceremonial banquets. Unlike hamburgers or hot dogs, public snack foods that only enter the home by way of the backyard, chicken was something you raised, killed, plucked, and ate when needed—a ready staple alongside the canned preserves that frequently accompanied it.

Even so, modern pressure cookers were high-tech. No one was going to start a fast-food empire using cast-iron skillets, even if those were the best way to cook chicken. (And they are. Calvin Trillin has memorably written, with complete justice, that "a fried chicken cook with a deep fryer is a sculptor working with mittens.")[7] It takes too long to make chicken in a pan, and even the most colossal version hammered out by a southern smithy can only hold thirty pieces at a time at most. On the other hand, it's not as if the pressure cooker was the obvious option. A fast-food restaurant can make as much fried chicken as it wants in minimal time by the expedient of just throwing the chicken into a deep fryer, a giant tank of boiling oil that stays at constant temperature. In fact, that's what nearly every fast-food operation uses, and even Kentucky Fried Chicken, over the Colonel's most strident objections, used the technology to create Extra Crispy chicken—which, to his bafflement and dismay, soon sold nearly as well as Original Recipe. It seems not to have occurred to the Colonel to use a french-fry machine for his chicken. No doubt the excellence of the final product had a lot to do with it; pressure-cooker chicken is succulent and moist in a way that no open fryer's chicken can be, no matter how ingenious or assiduous the pretreatment.

The real significance of the pressure cooker, though, is how completely and utterly mechanical a way of cooking it is. The Colonel was, by all accounts, a wonderful cook, but he was a country cook, accustomed to doing everything by feel and intuition. When you make fried chicken, you put some shortening in the pan, or maybe some lard, or maybe both, or not, and you get it hot. You don't know how hot because there's no thermometer nearby, and you can't say how high a flame because chances are you are using a wood or coal stove. (The fire you get depends on how much you use and how clogged the flues are and how much fuel is left in the pile.) You put a little of this and a little of that in the breading—usually whatever you have in the kitchen—and make it cling with an "egg warsh." The fat is ready when it sizzles when the chicken goes in. You wait long enough for it to brown. How long is that? Who knows? It takes as long as it takes, and you know how long that is because you've done it a thousand times and watched your mother do it a thousand times before that. You flip it when it's brown, and you move the dark pieces in around the hot parts of the pan and the white pieces around the colder parts so they all come out just right together. That's how you made fried chicken in Kentucky in 1900, when Harland Sanders started doing it, and how you do it today, at home in the South.

The pressure cooker is another story. It's a closed, windowless prison, a black box, an isolation chamber. You can't see the chicken as it cooks in there, can't smell it, can barely hear it. There's a little jiggly thing that alerts you that the pressure is on, but you don't know how much pressure the chicken is getting. And since it's cooking in an unnatural way, both steaming and frying at the same time, there's no way to tell what the hell's going on with it based on your actual experience as a southern home cook. In truth, everything about southern fried chicken is absent from and alien to Kentucky Fried Chicken except for the fact that it's not trying to be southern, which, paradoxically, makes it real. The Colonel would not have served chicken he thought he couldn't be proud of; and if it was a little softer than the pan-fried variety, that was OK. Southern cooks are not too particular about these details; they tend not to get hung up on genre and definition. As long as it was great, the Colonel was happy. But the fact remains that pressure-cooker chicken is a modern, mechanical, commercial technology, and the Colonel's chicken was designed from the ground up as modern, mechanical, commercial technology. Everything about it was modern except the Colonel himself. That has been the genius of Kentucky Fried Chicken then and now. In the early going, the pressure cooker was as much of the pitch as the proprietary seasoned flour or the Colonel's image itself.

The instrument played a memorable role in the very first moment of franchising. When Sanders was still in business in Corbin, before any hint of highway rerouting had appeared in the air, he determined, for some reason nobody has been able to reconstruct, to go to Australia to cure himself of cursing. A group of Kentucky clergyman booked the flight, and so the Colonel thought he might as well go along.

A year earlier, he had attended the National Restaurant Association's annual convention in Chicago and met a nice couple named Pete and Arline Harman. They were from Utah and teetotalers, like the Colonel, which put them in select company at a convention of restaurant operators in 1950. The three ate several dinners together and talked about food and cooking, and the encounters ended with a friendly invitation to stop by if he was ever in Salt Lake City. The chances of Harland Sanders finding himself there were remote, but he was exactly the kind of person who would look them up. When the flight to Australia had a long layover in Salt Lake City, the Colonel called up Harman and asked to see him. Kentucky Fried Chicken was about to be conceived, though neither man knew it at the time.

Pete Harman remembers the Colonel's original pitch. When Harman mentioned that he needed a new product, the Colonel, who had just started to think about the possibility of sending his fried chicken out on the hedges and the highways, took notice. (Five years later the chicken would be his salvation; in 1950, it was still a sideline.) Like almost everyone, Harman, the owner of a successful restaurant in Salt Lake City, immediately liked the Colonel and got a kick out of his salty, avuncular ways. But going into business with him was another story. When the Colonel arrived he announced that he wanted to show Harman something.

"Pete, instead of you taking me up the canyon for dinner, I want to cook for you," the Colonel told him.

> He needed spices, he needed a pressure cooker, he needed chicken, and he needed a stove to cook on. They found spices and four whole chickens at Jake's grocery store. A pressure cooker was tracked down at [an employee's] home, and she was invited to come try the new kind of chicken with them at about 5:30 that evening. The Colonel was a whirlwind in the kitchen, but inadequate burners on the stove slowed him down. It took forever to boost the oil to the necessary 400 degrees. As time ticked away and stomachs growled, the chicken finally was ready and put in a hot cabinet for holding until dinner. . . . Finally, at 10:00 pm, the Colonel announced that dinner was ready and set out the food for his dubious hosts. "It looks like greasy restaurant chicken," Arline whispered to Pete while the Colonel fussed some more in the kitchen.[8]

Everything turned around after everyone tasted the chicken and, of course, the Colonel's famous gravy, combined with the old man's sales pitch, perfected after decades and decades of practice. The trip to Australia, while pleasant enough, had no effect whatsoever on the Colonel's "cussing."

Harman is the unheralded hero of the Kentucky Fried Chicken story, the company's virtual cofounder. A quiet and unassuming man, more than anyone else he was the architect of Kentucky Fried Chicken Inc. Harman was the one who thought of the name Kentucky Fried Chicken.[9] He conceived of Kentucky Fried Chicken as a stand-alone restaurant. He invented the bucket, which, after the Colonel himself, was the chain's most recognizable symbol. (What other food, from what other chain, comes in a bucket?) He created the slogan "finger-lickin' good," which was likewise synonymous with the brand for most of its history. He remained a top figure in the hierarchy of the company through all its corporate owners. He was the first franchisee and the man who, it was felt by many, knew the Colonel best professionally. He is not known to the public because nobody cares who thought of the bucket, just as nobody cares who invented the idea of making Kentucky Fried Chicken primarily a take-out restaurant—an innovation that had as much to do with the chain's success as anything else in the mobile, motorized 1960s. (For the record, it was the Colonel's daughter Margaret.) Harland Sanders thought to reinvent himself as "the Colonel" and convinced a guy he had met once to use his fried chicken recipe at his diner. For that he deserves his immortality. But it would be a mistake to consider Sanders the sole author of Kentucky Fried Chicken or to credit him with having found solutions for the enterprise's innumerable practical challenges. Although given to fits of frustration with the food he tasted at far-flung restaurants, he did not have it in him to oversee the chain's operations himself. Though he would periodically vent—sometimes even to the press—the truth is that he liked to show up in his white suit, talk about "his" chicken, and leave. Everyone was happy with the arrangement, especially the Colonel. Pete Harman was actually charged with making it all work.

One of the biggest challenges Harman faced was figuring out a way to use pressure cookers to produce chicken at one volume. Even a single-burner pot, such as the Colonel drove around with in his backseat, was trouble. But how to run the dozens it would take to do the chicken on a large scale? Because that was what Harman had in mind from the beginning. The chicken wasn't to be a single item buried in a menu; it was to be the star of his restaurant, illustrated with a large roadside image of the Colonel. But this infernal machine was as precarious, volatile, and unpredictable as the Colonel's temper—

another thing that made it an ideal symbol of the enterprise in the early days. For all their usefulness, the pressure cookers of the 1930s and '40s were, like so much else from that era, thrown together by any number of now-defunct factories, many only slightly more efficient than Oskar Schindler's. They tended to blow up, often sending deadly shrapnel in every direction, and in some cases, shooting their contents at murderous velocity as well. The Colonel's practice of putting hot oil and chicken into them gave many a diner owner pause, and if the magnificent bird that came out was well worth the risk (and the nickel), they often remembered the pressure cooker to the end of their days. "You danged old fool," one told him, "you're only supposed to cook green beans and the like in a pressure cooker. That thing's going to blow you from here to Kingdom Come some day."[10] On at least one occasion, the Colonel managed to set himself on fire.[11] The pressure cooker took some raw physical courage, too—another quality that separates Harland Sanders from the other businessmen who founded restaurant empires in America. (Did Ray Kroc ever stitch his own scalp after a car accident? Did Glen "Taco" Bell ever trade gunshots in Hell's Half-Acre?)

Harman didn't take much convincing after he tasted the Colonel's chicken recipe. He acted quickly and decisively. First, having decided to make Kentucky Fried Chicken the centerpiece of his restaurant, Harman's Cafe, he put an enormous sign with the words "Colonel Sanders' Kentucky Fried Chicken," written with the now-ubiquitous lettering, in the window. Harman then bought all the unused radio time available on the local station for a bargain-basement five hundred dollars. "If there was anything that got Kentucky Fried Chicken off the ground," he later remembered, "it was gambling on radio's unsold time. We had to change equipment practically every day for two weeks just to cook enough chicken to satisfy demand."[12]

The restaurant, already a success, became a profit machine, and subsequent restaurants followed. At each one Harman pushed Kentucky Fried Chicken harder. By the time the third restaurant opened up, an oversize image of the Colonel, white suit and all, was featured on the sign. Harman was a natural at the business. He saw that take-out was going to become more important in an increasingly motorized, mobile, suburban postwar society, so to-go meals, designed from the ground up, became a key part of the operations. (Though not the main focus; that was to come later.) The bucket was an effort to sell big orders to whole families and quickly became the sole focus of Harman's take-out business. He saw that television was becoming a dominant medium and committed to TV, even arranging to have a local station broadcast live from one of the newly opened restaurants. In one of the most conservative parts of the country, he came up with a profit-sharing plan for his employees when such an arrangement was unprecedented. He was also one of the first major restaurant operators to aggressively hire women as managers.

But Harman's most lasting insight was in seeing, as the McDonald brothers did at about the same time in California, that the sit-down restaurant was a waste of time and effort, not to mention money. Why go to all the trouble of having waitresses and dishwashers and porters and busboys and salads and hamburgers and all the rest of it when all anyone wanted was chicken and that to take out? Harman, like the McDonalds, had come up out of small diners and restaurants and assumed that more was better, that the personal touch counted, that people wanted to eat a meal together. Not so! All they wanted was a bucket of very good, highly seasoned, crusty but tender fried chicken in a bucket and to be on their way. This insight would eventually lead another Sanders protégé, Dave Thomas, to invent the drive-in window, but that was still years in the future.

In the late 1950s, after Sanders Court and Cafe finally gave up the ghost and freed the Colonel to put all his thunderous energies into spreading his chicken gospel, the business started to pick up. All those little restaurants—a diner here, a roadhouse there—selling his chicken and honoring their end of a handshake deal began to pay off. There were hundreds of them, and more every day, as prospective franchisees would take a pilgrimage to Shelbyville, where the Sanders family now lived in a big white house. There the Colonel would talk up a storm, put them up for the night, and then make an immense southern breakfast of country ham, red-eye gravy, biscuits, scrambled eggs, bacon, grits, various pastries, and the strong black coffee served in the South. The franchisees, however, didn't join Team Sanders because of his ham and gravy, legendary though that was. They joined because they could make money with Kentucky Fried Chicken. And as Kentucky Fried Chicken became a more streamlined corporate business in the years to come, with a massive advertising budget and a famous name, those profits got bigger still.

The experience of Earl and Winnifried Smalley was a typical one. In 1969 the *New York Times* ran a profile of the couple. In the years when the Colonel was still recruiting franchisees, they would have been ideal targets. Incredibly hardworking, both had been brought up on farms, like the Colonel. They slaved away at a tiny mom-and-pop restaurant in Warsaw, Indiana, that barely supported them. Earl worked sixty-five hours a week, getting up before dark to clean and prep the place; Winnifried worked forty-five hours and raised their children. From 1957 to 1963 the place grossed $45,000 to $55,000 a year; after expenses, the two made about $3,000 a year—*between the two of them.* A year or so later (the piece doesn't specify), Earl was introduced to the Colonel. By this time it was no easy feat to get a Kentucky Fried Chicken franchise, which was recognized as a gold mine. But the Smalleys were given the chance, and they sold the luncheonette for a piddling $800, less than the equipment was worth. "At least I made something," Earl told the newspaper. "There have been three guys in there since and they all went broke." They borrowed $20,000 to buy the franchise and within ten months had paid it off. The first year they earned $30,000, literally ten times what they made previously.

Multiply the story of the Smalleys by ten thousand and you

begin to get the picture of what Kentucky Fried Chicken meant to its partners. The image everyone has of a fast-food "empire" is that of a vast and homogeneous pattern of clones filling up a map like cancer cells and erasing all tradition at the behest of self-interested corporate forces. This isn't entirely inaccurate, and there's no question that any number of small, rural institutions, very much in the vein of Sanders Cafe, have now been replaced by Kentucky Fried Chicken franchises. On the other hand, there is something so wrong, so un-American about the working poverty of people like the Smalleys. How could someone work that hard in a business so necessary, so woven into the daily life of their town, and not have anything to show for it? These weren't factory workers or migrant field hands or sweatshop drudges; these were property owners who had clawed their way to middle age and still could barely make enough to live on. All they wanted was a chance. It wasn't the Warsaw Chamber of Commerce that gave it to them or the Rotarians or the Great Society; it was the Colonel.

Moreover, as would become increasingly clear in the years ahead, it was the franchisees for whom he had the most sympathy. They were the ones sweating in the kitchens, striving away, while in Louisville a group of high-handed businessmen reaped the profits, just as they were reaping the profits from his life's work. (Of course, when he ventured into a Kentucky Fried Chicken franchise that served "his" food in less than satisfactory form—which was pretty much all of them—he would berate them mercilessly.) The franchisees had an ongoing relationship with the corporation, which began as warm and personal, became merely cooperative later, and by the 1980s would become deeply adversarial. The company gave with one hand and took with the other. On one side, Kentucky Fried Chicken gave them their fortunes and their livelihoods, not to mention the secret central substance, the Colonel's unique seasoned flour—the chain's sole claim of distinction in a murderously crowded field. Then, too, the corporation matched their advertising and marketing contributions so both were partners in promoting the brand. Meanwhile, the company got a lot from the franchisees, too. They were its lifeblood. All of the company's revenues came from them, and they weren't employees. They were partners who needed to be treated politically rather than ordered around. The only remedy against their disobedience was to threaten removal of their franchise, which would just result in losing all the money they brought in. Eventually the company would own thousands of stores itself, but in the beginning, every Kentucky Fried Chicken restaurant was private property. The owner could lock the door and tell the CEO to go to hell at any time, and this did happen from time to time. At the same time, the company retained operating control, which was something a business rarely gets to keep when running on outside capital. It took money from the franchisees, but they didn't have to give back a single bit of stock or the power it represented.

At the same time, the franchisees understood the business better than did the chain's executives in their big white headquarters in Louisville. The franchisees were closer to the ground. When the two groups disagreed, the company could be brought to a standstill, as happened in the 1990s when Kentucky Fried Chicken, under a series of indifferent corporate owners, milked the chain for profits while ignoring the views of the most experienced franchisees, including Pete Harman himself. Harman, unthinkably, even became a plaintiff in a suit filed by the franchisees against the company during those darkest days.

In the late 1950s, though, there was no Kentucky Fried Chicken corporation. There was a "family" of franchisees, very few of whom had dedicated Kentucky Fried Chicken restaurants. They were a loose confederation bound by a recipe and a handshake deal. There was Pete Harman with a handful of stores in distant Utah, the forerunners of all future Kentucky Fried Chicken outlets. There was the Colonel, and there was Claudia. And that was it. The franchisees sent their checks in on the honor system, and the Colonel cashed them when he got around to it. By 1960 he had more than two hundred outlets for his chicken, extending all the way into the Great White North of Canada. He personally had a small staff including an accountant, and he had a gold Rolls Royce with "KENTUCKY FRIED CHICKEN" painted on both sides. A short time later Colonel's Foods, a subsidiary company, came along to oversee production of various food-service items like sauces and breading, followed by the sad but inevitable end to the handshake era.

The Colonel wasn't content to just cash the checks, though; he was still a berserker in his pursuit of quality control and "doing things the right way." He demanded as a condition of application that all new franchisees grant him the right to inspect their restaurants with the understanding that he could withdraw their franchises if they departed from his decrees. This could, in theory, have been anything from using powdered eggs in the breading wash to swapping mashed potatoes for french fries in certain markets. The Colonel seems not to have exercised his excommunication prerogative often, happily. John Ed Pearce describes how overwhelmed the Colonel was in this era:

> He was now having real trouble franchising, policing his franchisees, running the Shelbyville headquarters and distribution facility, teaching at the regional schools he was setting up [to teach operations], checking on the books, hiring new people, and grappling with taxes and corporate laws. He and Claudia began to wonder if they would ever get to relax, travel and enjoy what they had built.[13]

At the end of his rope, Sanders turned to an old friend, John Y. Brown, then one of the state's most powerful lawyers. He needed help. Brown, enjoying a profitable practice after enduring years in Kentucky's rough-and-tumble political scene, declined to come on board. But his son, John Jr., had just gone into practice, and, well, why didn't the Colonel go on over and see him?

3

KENTUCKY FRIED CHICKEN INC.

John Y. Brown Jr., the former governor of Kentucky, is invariably described as "Kennedyesque." The appellation isn't that far off, or at least it wasn't in Brown's youth. Handsome, charismatic, a famous playboy and bon vivant, and a natural in the game of politics, he also inherited a potent political legacy: Brown's father, John Sr., had been a major force in Kentucky politics for two generations. John Jr. got around to taking the top position in the state, from 1979 to 1983, and even considered a run at the presidency—but not before creating Kentucky Fried Chicken Inc., marrying Miss America, owning three professional basketball teams, and creating a legendary reputation as a high-stakes poker player and ladies' man. He liked to have a nip of Kentucky bourbon now and again. He was on easy terms with the most powerful people in every sector of society. He was cultivated and genteel and had led a smooth and sheltered life as one of the most privileged young people in a famously plutocratic state.[1] No man could have been more alien to Harland Sanders.

It seems unlikely that the seventy-three-year-old Colonel, therefore, would have chosen so willingly to go into business with Brown, who had no prior experience in business or restaurants. "I knew that he felt I had led a different sort of life than he had, that I came from a different background," Brown later said. "But he liked me."[2] There seems no doubt that the Colonel was attracted to, and even a little intimidated by, Brown's social ease, assurance, and gentility, all qualities Sanders lacked to one degree or another. The two had been introduced before the Colonel came to him for legal counsel; appropriately enough, the two bluegrass titans first met at the Kentucky Derby in 1963, with the Colonel resplendent in his whites and Brown, sportsman and scion, as in his element as any man could ever hope to be.

When Brown did come to talk business with the Colonel, he paid court the right way, visiting him in the big white house in Shelbyville. Brown was a natural salesman, too. He had an effortless gift for getting people to buy things, from vacuum cleaners to encyclopedias, and it didn't take him long to realize that he wanted to sell himself to the Colonel. "He showed me a big pile of checks that his franchisees had sent him—he had over six hundred by then—and they were made out for a hundred, two hundred, three hundred dollars. I had no idea there was that much money in his chicken business."[3] Brown's first thought was about neither spice mixes nor pressure cookers. "What kind of a sales force do you have?" he asked.

"Hell, I got no sales force," the Colonel snapped back. "If people want to sell my chicken, they can come to me now. I don't have to go to them." Brown remembers, "I said to myself, 'Brown, you better pull up a chair and sit in.'" Given the obvious need each man had for the other, they ought to have joined forces then and there, the Colonel providing the product, the image, and the authenticity, and Brown incorporating the business into the matrix of modern business practice and cutting himself in for a hefty slice in the process. The two men were perfect partners, and there was deep warmth between them that persisted for many years, even in the Colonel's irascible eighties. But Sanders wasn't ready to part with his newfound business so painfully earned. Instead, they decided to open a barbecue restaurant together. "The Colonel was still pretty possessive about his chicken business, but he never stopped thinking about new projects," Brown says, "and he had it in his head that he wanted to open a barbecue. So we opened a barbecue."[4]

The barbecue business is incredibly challenging, requiring major capital investment in all kinds of specialty equipment, and Brown borrowed money from Jack Massey, a Louisville investor. The Porky Pig House, as it was called, went nowhere fast: as the Colonel had pointed out in colorful language, Brown knew nothing about restaurants and now was trying to run a complicated, capital-heavy business on a shoestring. But he had access to money; that was what he brought to the deal. So when the Colonel complained to Brown that he was having trouble keeping up with the costs of supplying pressure cookers, seasoned flour, paper products, and the like to all his franchisees spread around the continent, Brown took Massey up to Shelbyville to see the Colonel. It was now 1964, a year into the barbecue business. The idea was that Brown and Massey would buy into Kentucky Fried Chicken. Then the Colonel would have access to some serious operating capital, and they would be in on the ground floor of an aggressively expanding business.

The Colonel, having never been really successful as a businessman, having been in debt a good part of his life, and having a bone-deep distaste for people who had never done the kind of hard work that he had mastered at age twelve, was skeptical. He saw all "moneymen" as swindlers, usurers, and was notably gruff, even for him. He acted strangely uneasy. Brown remembers that he was "constantly muttering, pulling his moustache, stuff like that." The young man couldn't figure out what it was all about: "He said he needed money, and I was bringing a person to him who could help. It was very upsetting." After much delay, the Colonel finally came out with it: "Let me tell you right now," he said, "there ain't no slick-talking sonofabitch going to come in here and buy my company out from under me. Nosir!"[5]

Both men were shocked. Neither had even considered the

idea of buying Kentucky Fried Chicken. Brown had just borrowed a lot of money for the Porky Pig House; he was still thinking about getting the place profitable so as to pay it back. Massey had come along to Shelbyville as a favor to Brown, whom he considered something of a protégé. The idea of going into the fried chicken business was the furthest thing from their minds, or so they claimed afterward.

Harland Sanders, on the other hand, had a lot of good reasons for selling Kentucky Fried Chicken. Brown came around to the idea pretty quickly and made haste to suggest it to him over the next few weeks with varying degrees of gentleness. He was in his seventies now, an old man; shouldn't he enjoy his golden years, hmm? Hadn't he earned the right to relax a little? And then, what about the business? If he left it in the hands of the franchisees, as was his plan up until his odd outburst, the loose network of restaurants would inevitably fracture in discord. Neither of the Colonel's daughters was interested in taking over the business, and of course Harland Jr. was many years in the grave now.

Beyond all this, there was a single reason above all the others, and it was this one that carried the day. He simply wasn't able to run the business by himself. He could sell and promote anything under the sun, and he could make chicken like a champ. But he was no businessman, not at this age and not on this scale. "I'd been in business for myself for more than thirty-five years at one thing or another," the Colonel later wrote, looking back at the fateful decision.

> During that time I'd seen successes turn to failures for reasons that were out of my control. Now I had built up the most successful business I ever had singlehanded—startin' from scratch when I was sixty-five. And that had taken only nine years.
>
> *Why the hell am I sellin' out now?* I asked myself.
>
> Then I realized how the popularity of Kentucky Fried Chicken was growin' right over me and mashin' me flat.[6]

The Colonel took his time making up his mind. He was genuinely ambivalent, even with all the good reasons Brown had given him. There would be no going back or starting over after he made the sale. A lifelong believer in the gospel of work, he would have no real reason for being, or so he feared, if he sailed. (At the age of eighty-eight he testified before a congressional subcommittee, telling them that "retiring is the awfullest thing in the world."[7])He temporized, delayed, had momentary changes of heart and just as swift reversals, all while Brown and Massey, who had been persuaded by Brown that Kentucky Fried Chicken was a gold mine, twisted in the wind. "It was a stressful time, believe me," Brown says now.[8]

In many ways it was a good deal for the Colonel. He would get $2 million in cash, more than he ever dreamed of, plus $40,000 a year to work as a goodwill ambassador, "the living symbol of Kentucky Fried Chicken." (Later this would be upped to $75,000.) He didn't take any stock, for tax reasons, but that didn't bother him; he now had more money than he could ever spend. Cash was what he preferred anyway, cash on the barrelhead: $500,000 up front, payable within two months, and the rest paid over a five-year period. In other ways, the deal wasn't that good. The Colonel, accustomed to a lifetime of handshake arrangements and leaving "the paperwork" for later, had agreed, he thought, to a sale in principal and had a few lawyer friends look at the contract. After he signed it, he found that the money wasn't as amazing as he thought; in fact, given the payout schedule, it was less than he was making before the sale. His salary for a busy full-time job as the face of the brand was a relative pittance, and the company would even get to keep his residual royalties! But there was nothing he could do. "Father had only himself to blame," his daughter Margaret would later say. "Father's hands were tied, and his lousy salary was hardly enough to compensate for the exhaustion he experienced from flying around the world making commercials."[9] Worse still, he had signed away the right to use his own name and image on any other business for the rest of his life.

Harland P. Sanders, the Colonel. Courtesy of KFC Corporation.

The office of Colonel Sanders is kept to this day exactly as he left it.
Courtesy of KFC Corporation.

Harland Sanders, circa 1920: a young businessman on the rise.
Courtesy of KFC Corporation.

The Colonel's original pressure cooker, which is kept by KFC as a sacred relic. It was in this vessel that the first batch of Kentucky Fried Chicken was cooked. Courtesy of KFC Corporation.

The kitchen at Sanders' gas station: the genesis of Kentucky Fried Chicken. Courtesy of KFC Corporation.

Sanders Court & Cafe—it might have been remembered as just another piece of roadside Americana, but for the Colonel's subsequent career. Courtesy of KFC Corporation.

The Sanders Cafe in the mid-1960s, halfway through its metamorphosis into KFC. Courtesy of KFC Corporation.

Sanders Cafe, in Corbin Kentucky, as it looks today. Courtesy of KFC Corporation.

Harland Sanders in middle age, before the suit and the white beard.
Courtesy of KFC Corporation.

The Colonel in his pre–white suit period. Courtesy of KFC Corporation.

The first public appearance of Kentucky Fried Chicken—at Pete Harman's
Dew Drop Inn in Utah. Courtesy of KFC Corporation.

An early Kentucky Fried Chicken restaurant. Courtesy of KFC Corporation.

Colonel Sanders, man and icon. Courtesy of KFC Corporation.

Part of the Kentucky Fried Chicken recipe was breaking the
chicken down into nine pieces. Courtesy of KFC Corporation.

The Colonel demonstrates how to fry in a pressure cooker. Note the Band-aids from grease splatters. Courtesy of KFC Corporation.

An elderly Colonel demonstrates a fine point of pressure-cookery.
Courtesy of KFC Corporation.

The Colonel and a typical Rube Goldberg–like fryer. Courtesy of KFC Corporation.

The Colonel as a guest on What's My Line, *prior to his apotheosis.*
Courtesy of KFC Corporation.

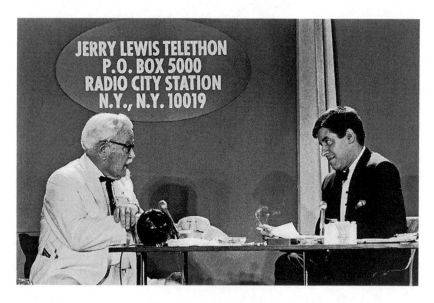

The Colonel and Jerry Lewis trade quips on the latter's Labor Day telethon.
Courtesy of KFC Corporation.

Always an admirer of beauty, the Colonel pays his respects to the one and only Zsa Zsa Gabor. Courtesy of KFC Corporation.

Painter Norman Rockwell was prevailed upon late in his life to paint the Colonel by the Colonel's protégé, engineer Winston Shelton. It took some persistence; in the end, Rockwell complied with the condition that the Colonel remove his glasses. Courtesy of KFC Corporation.

Harland Sanders lived long enough to enjoy the sight of his own memorial legacy. How many men can say the same? Courtesy of KFC Corporation.

A modern KFC, complete with an idealized icon of the chain's founder.
Courtesy of KFC Corporation.

The Colonel in his last years. Courtesy of KFC Corporation.

The problem was that the Colonel wasn't just making decisions on behalf of himself but rather his "family" of franchisees—a term he actually took seriously. Certainly there could be no sale without speaking to Pete Harman and Kenny King of Cleveland, the two biggest and earliest franchisees. To his surprise and possible dismay, they were all in favor of it. The major franchisees were going to get big chunks of stock, and the Colonel let himself believe that they would watch out for the other franchisees and the quality of the product, having been chicken men themselves, unlike shady moneymen who never knew what it was to mop up a restaurant at six in the morning.

The deal finally got done on February 18, 1964. The Colonel, in one of his most expansive moments, made this written promise to Brown and Massey:

> It is my intention to deliver to you the best and most conscientious service I can render, consistent with my health, as long as I remain on your payroll . . . the business is yours to operate as you please, and I will never be critical to anyone other than you two about how you operate it. Anything that I suggest to you would be merely a suggestion, and no hard feelings on my part if they are not taken.[10]

There's no question that Sanders believed this at the time, but no one with even a passing knowledge of his character could ever have believed that he could abide by it. This was a man who thought nothing of visiting strangers' homes and running into the kitchen with a drill to bore holes in the gas range, a man who had made a lifelong habit of swearing at employees, his own and those of unlucky restaurant owners, and knocking any nearby surface with the end of his cane to indicate his displeasure at imperfectly cooked scrambled eggs. There was no way that the presence of this temperamental, stubborn, opinionated individual was going to be easy to control; the question was merely how volatile an asset the Colonel would be for the newly formed corporation.

And make no mistake: he was their chief asset. As Brown says, "The Colonel wasn't just the face of the company; he *was* the company. I used to tell people inside the company, there's two reasons we're all rich: because the Colonel came up with a good product, and because he looked good on that sign."[11] For Brown, the Colonel was more than the face of the franchise; he was almost mythic. "He wasn't just a trademark. He wasn't just somebody that an adman had made up, like Aunt Jemima, Colonel Morton, or Betty Crocker. He was a real, live human being and a colorful, attractive, persuasive one. My job was to get him before the American people and let him sell his own product."[12]

With the Colonel established as a living mascot, a flesh-and-blood Uncle Ben, Brown was able to mobilize his peerless sales ability to get more and more franchisees signed up. Brown was done with having Kentucky Fried Chicken be an item on someone else's menu. Now every restaurant would be a freestanding one with identical signage, architecture, and maximized efficiency. And every one would be built from the ground up with an eye toward take-out. This innovation was currently powering McDonald's to unheard-of success, the hamburger company having ridden the postwar baby boom to glory. The prosperity World War II brought to the country produced an unprecedented demographic explosion, and an expanding "crabgrass frontier" of new suburbs was coming into being. Those suburbs were largely occupied by young families of exactly the kind that might need a bucket of chicken for dinner one night a week or even more than one night a week.

Another thing about these families was that they all had cars; that was how they could live in the suburbs, why suburbs existed. The new Kentucky Fried Chicken outlets that Brown had in mind would, like Pete Harman's operations in Utah, be totally dedicated not just to fried chicken but to the Colonel's brand. They would feature the Colonel's "mug" as the central visual identity of the place, with every element from a red-and-white color scheme to a mansard roof with a rotating bucket overhead dedicated to beaming his image to everyone within visual range. But unlike Harman's restaurants, they wouldn't be primarily urban affairs catering to a dine-in clientele. The Colonel's daughter Margaret, who owned a hereditary title to all franchises in Florida, started the first one, in Jacksonville, and it did so well that it became the template for future operations. Why not? It was so cheap to have a take-out restaurant: no waiters, no big building, no dishwashers, no linen—just chicken in boxes and buckets, and plenty of it.

Now the Colonel was rich at last, rich beyond his wildest imaginings, and he had a license to spend all his time "colonel-ing." The white suit went on for good sometime in the early '60s. Slowly but surely the country began to learn about him. Duncan Hines notwithstanding, he wasn't well known on a national level, not yet. Kentucky Fried Chicken, for one thing, was still a regional chain. For another, there were still no plans to start doing national TV advertising. At first, there was no paid advertising at all. The Colonel got it for free by appearing on talk shows.

In the Colonel's first national television appearance he was still so obscure that he was chosen as the Mystery Guest on a 1963 episode of *What's My Line?*, a popular quiz show of the 1950s and '60s. The panelists on the show were allowed to pose a certain number of broad queries that if insufficient would lead to a cash prize for the guest. Naturally, no prominent public figure would be invited as the guest. The Colonel, in full whites, appeared before the panel, which asked him such baffled questions as "Is your product anything I might use?" (Arlene Francis), "Is your product a fruit or a vegetable?" (Dorothy Kilgallen), and "Is it ever used in connection with that marvelous drink, a mint julep?" (Martin Gabel).

The panelists were unable to puzzle out what the Colonel made and appeared skeptical when he described its finger-licking-good qualities. "How many spices is it . . . ?" host John Charles Daly asked the Colonel, and the guest had a ready answer. He inserted a quick statement about nine hundred restaurants and "a patented frying method" and wrapped up, all in the same breath, by telling the viewing audience, "Wherever you see a picture of this mug of mine, you know you're going to get good food, at least good chicken." There was polite laughter, and the Colonel was sent on his way.

Watching the clip today, one can't help finding it somewhat surreal. How is it possible that the panelists had no idea who Colonel Sanders was? (A similar question on the other side of history hit KFC in the form of its 2010 survey.) The answer is obvious, in retrospect; he wasn't on TV yet. Not that the high-brows who cross-examined him would have watched much TV in any case or admitted to it if they had. But when a short time later "the Colonel" became universally known, it was nei-ther because of the excellence of his chicken nor his "mug" on signs from coast to coast. No, the engine of his fame, of almost all fame in America at the time, was television. And the Colonel turned out to be a natural for TV.

Other spots and cameos followed. Brown, showing a pre-scient awareness of the power of television, brought in Stan Lewis, a Madison Avenue ad executive, to get the Colonel into the public mind. In 1967 the Colonel appeared in two not-so-memorable movies—as an irate customer who bangs his cane on a hotel desk in Jerry Lewis' *The Big Mouth* and as the owner of a fried chicken restaurant in Herschell Gordon Lewis' *Blast Off Girls*. A few years later Sanders would appear in two even worse movies, *The Phynx* and *Hell's Bloody Devils*, as himself.

On the small screen he was a regular presence. He appeared on *The Tonight Show* with a box supposedly containing his two million dollars. On Merv Griffin's show an actor walked up and down the aisles looking for "that Colonel that stole my wife," and when the man found the Colonel, not at all inconspicuous in his white suit, his quarry high-tailed it down the aisle fol-lowed by ushers carrying buckets of chicken, which he then proceeded to hand out to the crowd.

The Colonel was a big hit on television, much to the sur-prise of Stan Lewis, John Y. Brown, and everybody else. It was conceivable that he would get nervous, flub his lines, or otherwise flinch at the thought of appearing before so many people at once. Also, everyone was aware that the Colonel, despite his vitality, was an old man: by the time of his first appearance on *What's My Line?* he was already seventy-three years old and looked like the guy on the bucket. But as they found out, he was able to adopt his lifelong sales gift to the camera without too much trouble, even to the extent of impromptu joshing around with various talk-show hosts. He wasn't the gifted performer some of his hagiographers make him out to be; at his best the Colonel was a somewhat wooden performer, albeit a likable one.

By 1969 his TV persona was well established and perfectly presented in a commercial. The viewer peers through the window on a rainy night to see him seated in a rocker with a little girl on his knee. "I'm Colonel Harland Sanders, and I'd like to tell you a little bit about my Kentucky Fried Chicken," he says in a quick, clipped monotone. A prim young woman in an old-fashioned blouse affixed with a cameo says from the dining room, "Ain't you coming?" As the Colonel sends the little girl along, saying, "You go ahead, honey, I want to talk to these folks a little bit longer," he has launched headlong into his practiced patter. "Now there's only one way to cook Kentucky Fried Chicken, and that's my way. We always use plump young broilers, always fresh, never frozen. [Cut to images of the children eating chicken pieces and licking their fingers.] Each piece is dipped into an 'egg warsh' and then seasoned flour [Dad takes a bite] in which we have the eleven different spices and herbs for flavor." Then, without pausing, he says, "One more thing, folks: it's the only way you're ever going to get chicken that's finger-licking good, and I'd be mighty proud to have you try Colonel Sanders' Kentucky Fried Chicken. Mighty proud." He rises from his chair. "Now excuse me a minute, please," he says, shuffling off toward the dining room, where his red-haired, cameo-wearing daughter, an older version of Wendy, is licking her fingers. The sight finally rouses the somnolent Colonel from his trance, and he becomes, for the first time, animated: "Hey, looka there! Didn't I tell you it was finger-licking good? Heh

heh heh," he laughs, walking with his cane toward the table. A melodious baritone rolls over the scene, singing "Kentucky Fried Chicken. If you want Kentucky Fried Chicken, you'll have to visit me . . . ," and the words "Visit the Colonel" appear at the bottom of the screen.

The message is clear enough—the Colonel represents old-time values. He's bathed in the warm light of a fireplace, the familial hearth keeping his kin warm on a cold and rainy night. We come in out of the rain to see him; as the commercial begins, the camera is very much on the outside looking in. "Yes," it seems to say, "you live in a grossly inhospitable modern age filled with Vietnam, hippies, and skyrocketing meat prices—but there's still room for you here at the Colonel's table." For one thing, the spot misses no opportunity to remind us of the Colonel's role as a living bridge to that antebellum idyll and ourselves. He's physically between us and the Sanders family (with the chicken keeping them all together). And he's addressing us with familiarity ("I want to talk to these folks a while longer") even though we've just met ("I'm Colonel Harland Sanders. . . ."). All his talk of plump broilers and "egg warsh" is merely a distraction from the main attraction, which is the sight of the family all eating fried chicken together in a genteel setting, licking their fingers as they do so. The Colonel even shares a laugh with us over it at the end; it's as if we've somehow bonded with him.

It's the end of the commercial that most underscores just how important Sanders was to the whole enterprise. Up until the last shot of the commercial, we've existed entirely under his spell in a carefully art-directed vision of antebellum comfort. Colonel Sanders was the main thing Kentucky Fried Chicken had going for it. As the exterior shot shows at the end—of a big Kentucky Fried Chicken restaurant surrounded by a parking lot—nothing about the product could be further from this sentimental scene. Kentucky Fried Chicken was the cutting edge of a new kind of restaurant deliberately created to sever all the last bonds between private and public dining. Minimal options, no servers, a stark space without even a shred of linen, and a business completely geared toward speed and take-out orders via a battery of high-tech pressure cookers—that was the reality of Kentucky Fried Chicken. It was the power of the Colonel's image to coat this pill in the sentimental signs of the Old South, of hospitality with a human face. That is part of what makes the transition from the real Colonel to the illustrated face rotating atop a tower such a profound juxtaposition. In future commercials, great pains would be taken to make Kentucky Fried Chicken restaurants look almost as friendly and warmly lit as the fantasy home featured in the commercial.

Of course, the real life of Kentucky Fried Chicken was far from a family business, either in fact or in spirit. The initial public offering, ennobled by the Colonel's presence on the floor of the New York Stock Exchange, was an enormous hit. He bought the first hundred shares of Kentucky Fried Chicken at ten dollars a share and after a series of splits found himself selling them at a whopping four hundred dollars a share. Everyone wanted a piece of the new chain, and, at least at first, the confidence did not seem misplaced: within two years the chain opened more than 1,000 stores, 861 in 1968 alone, and brought in over $100 million in total sales.

The effect on Kentucky Fried Chicken's infrastructure was a kind of irrational exuberance. Twenty-one employees were made "instant millionaires" as a result of their stock holdings, and nobody, including even John Y. Brown, had the slightest idea how to run a multimillion-dollar, transnational corporation. The general feeling seemed to be that they had "made it" and that they ought to just keep the money coming in by opening more Kentucky Fried Chicken restaurants.

The executives "became a bunch of prima donnas," Brown recollects, adding that his wife at the time urged him to fire everybody.[13] But firing large sectors of the staff just as they had accomplished a great feat after much labor, endless hours, and great personal sacrifice was no more Brown's way than it would have been the Colonel's. The plain fact was that Brown, every bit as much as his goodwill ambassador, was an accidental traveler, a sharp-eyed opportunist who happened to see a chance to do something big and tapped into the immense forces transforming America in the 1960s. A number of these have been mentioned already: the baby boom, the National Highway Act, the growth of the suburbs, car culture, and the like. A far more important one, though, and less frequently mentioned by historians was absorption of restaurant chains by big business.

The idea of a fried chicken restaurant being traded on the New York Stock Exchange would have seemed patently insane to anyone in the 1920s, when it was understood that the proper concerns of large corporations were vast and impersonal enterprises like railroads, mining, and steel. All that changed when McDonald's went public in 1965. It was an immediate success, splitting over and over again. As a result, soon every major chain became attractive to large corporations seeking profitable businesses to fit into their portfolios. Often these were food companies like Pillsbury, which acquired Burger King in 1967, and General Foods, which bought Burger Chef the same year. And why not? These were national chains run in the most stable, modern management methods, usually by graduates of the country's top business and law schools. These were no longer isolated enterprises run by one or another regional mogul; they were genuinely national businesses. That was what made them valuable. But that had nothing whatever to do with Harland Sanders—or, for that matter, his chicken.

Brown was ahead of the curve in intuiting that the business could become that big; still, its success surprised him as much as anybody. Just as Harland Sanders had been a successful but by no means iconic motel and restaurant owner in the years before fast food took over the country, Brown should have been a successful Louisville businessman with a Cadillac, a share in a thoroughbred horse, and, maybe, a fast track in Louisville politics. It was in no way through his own conscious agency that he had become the head of a giant corporation—a corporation, in fact, that had no real long-term plans and no senior management to speak of.

Nor was Brown the sole owner. Jack Massey, the Nashville investor who had made Kentucky Fried Chicken possible by laying out most of the money, knew even less than Brown about the restaurant business, fast-food chains or otherwise, and was so unconscious of the Kentucky Fried Chicken brand that he insisted, over the Colonel's most profane objections, that the headquarters be moved to his home state of Tennessee. Massey claimed that the move was to help attract stockholders—a ludicrous argument in retrospect. Nobody goes to Nashville to attract investors unless they are starting a country-and-western band. The Colonel, predictably, was devastated. Previously, the headquarters had been an office adjacent to his home in Shelbyville. He and Claudia had launched the business there. It was a cold, hard reality for him to face, and he didn't take to it well. Sanders had despised Massey pretty much from the first. The move cemented his loathing. He was therefore primed and paranoid and all too ready to believe a rumor he heard that one of Massey's people had suggested getting rid of the Colonel by cutting his pension and thus maneuvering him into quitting.[14]

The idea was so absurd, especially in those boom years of the company's success, that it's hard to imagine it could really have happened. On the other hand, it's not inconceivable. Sanders was, in fact, a royal pain in the ass, and his antipathy toward Massey was fully reciprocated. Still, no one at Kentucky Fried Chicken can say who the person was or what he or she might have been thinking. It may well be that someone vented in a meeting after one of Sanders' tongue lashings that there must be some way to get rid of him. Whether the idea was ever seriously proposed, the Colonel heard about it somehow and at the worst possible time: just before he was to address the first convention of franchisees, more than a thousand of them, gathered to pledge their unity and fealty to the new leadership. When the Colonel showed up in a black suit, Brown knew he was in for trouble.

The Colonel proceeded to excoriate management for more than forty minutes. They had forgotten the people who had made them what they were. They were squeezing the franchisees, thinking only about the short term. They were destroying the company that he and his "family" had built. The food wasn't as good and was getting worse, thanks to their newfangled innovations and their modernization plans and their corporate plotting and moneymaking schemes. The Colonel went on and on. Massey, who was seated on his right, turned red and was burning up. Brown was covered with sweat. It was a dark moment and, really, one of the Colonel's most ignoble acts. Massey and Brown had paid him a generous amount for his business, and he had sworn in the most earnest and solemn terms never to criticize them; now he was attempting to humiliate them publicly in the most awkward possible place and time. Whether or not he believed or pretended to believe that the company was looking to get him out by means of some sinister pension scheme, it was utterly out of character to plan out such an attack.

Brown was especially embarrassed. "I saw everything going up in smoke," he would later tell John Ed Pearce. "Here, in what was supposed to be our hour of victory, our leader, our symbol, had turned against us. And I knew good and well that if these people believed him, if he left us and turned them against us, our company was shot."[15] After the Colonel had exhausted his ire, Brown stood up. As he reconstructed his off-the-cuff remarks for Pearce and future interviewers (his account of it to me was almost word for word the same), this was Brown's response:

> What we have just heard shows why we have one of the great companies of the world, and why it is going to be even greater. For this man here, who founded it, is an artist, and like all great artists, he's a perfectionist. He founded this company on the desire not just for profit but for excellence . . . The Colonel wants us to keep up to his standards. What we represent is the Colonel's dream. It really is a dream, and it's up to us to make that dream come true. It may be that in

our rapid growth, in our drive to organize this fast-growing company along the lines of order and efficiency that are fair to everyone, we have somehow slipped from following your standards, Colonel. But, Colonel, let me say this: when you sold this company to us, you asked us to be fair and honorable, and we have been. We haven't had a single lawsuit. There is not one single person who can say that we haven't honored every promise, every contract we have made. If there is anyone here who has any complaint, who feels he has been treated unfairly, we haven't heard of it, and we want to hear of it.[16]

The Colonel, still thinking the crowd was with him, grabbed the microphone and asked for a show of hands. None went up. His coup had failed. Brown, sensing his victory in hand, proceeded to the strongest part of his counterargument, which, born salesman that he was, he had held in reserve: the unquestionable litany of Kentucky Fried Chicken's financial successes—the immense sales figures, the growth, the profits being seen by franchisees from both operations and stock. He ended by turning to his vanquished attacker and saying, "Colonel, you're still our leader. You'll always be our leader. And I give you my word that we're going to make this company all you want it to be and more." The room erupted in applause. Most of the crowd knew the Colonel well and saw his intemperate attack as just hotheadedness. None were prepared to take arms against the company that was making them rich, however. Even the Colonel knew he had been in the wrong. "Well, John, you did a good job last night," he told Brown.[17] The two men never spoke of it again and even remained friendly, although the Colonel always believed that he had been swindled, or pretended to believe it, anyway.[18] Irascible but essentially good-natured, he simply found it hard to hold a grudge, particularly against the charming and deferential Brown, who continued to treat the Colonel as a father and to act as his advocate internally at the corporation. There was no doubt, though, who was boss. Within Kentucky Fried Chicken, the showdown had a galvanizing effect, removing any doubt of who was in charge and placing the Colonel, then and forever, in his powerless role as goodwill ambassador for a company he founded but no longer controlled. His dream, the American Dream, of fame and fortune regardless of rank had come true; but the price of it had been the erasure of his identity. And he knew it.

4

≡ BARBARIANS AT THE GATE ≡

By 1969, five years after the sale, the average Kentucky Fried Chicken restaurant had annual gross sales of nearly a quarter of a million dollars. Many were double that. The stock price at its highest was more than fifty-five dollars—an astronomical sum by the standards of the time. More than three thousand stores were in the system, with more opening every week. The company passed Howard Johnson as the leading food dispenser in America, excluding only the Army, the Navy, and the U.S. Department of Agriculture's school lunch program. These were inspiring numbers and, one would have thought, more than enough to keep Brown and his troops busy. The company was still a small one, with most of the major decisions being made by Brown and his immediate subordinates (usually including a courtesy consultation with the Living Legend) in their Nashville headquarters. The stock price was based on the rate of expansion that Kentucky Fried Chicken had seen in the 1960s, when the country was virgin territory and such rivals as Kentucky Fried Chicken found were small, poorly organized, and late to the game.

No entity as singularly and spectacularly successful as Kentucky Fried Chicken could fail to inspire imitators. Much as the novel success of White Castle earlier in the century inspired a nationwide wave of clones with variant DNA—White Tower, Blue Castle, Royal Castle, White Manna, White Diamond— Kentucky Fried Chicken inspired a flurry of get-rich-quick schemes looking to cash in on the fried-chicken craze. There was All-Pro Chicken, Chicken Hut, Maryland Fried Chicken, Ozark Fried Chicken with "Miss Alma's Recipe," Cock-A-Doodle of America, Pail-O-Chicken, and Wife-Saver Chicken. Various celebrities, too, were encouraged by their accountants to lend their names to chicken chains in the hope that a ready-made icon might rival the Colonel's all-powerful brand recognition. Country music proved to be a profitable breeding ground for these chains: Grand Ole Opry superstar Minnie Pearl and crooner Eddy Arnold sold their share of birds, and later, when John Y. Brown wanted back into the chicken business, he cast his eye about for another white-bearded deity and found him in the leonine Kenny Rogers. Soul-music stars were also a natural match for chicken chains, given the dish's special African American provenance so painstakingly unacknowledged by the Colonel. Mahalia Jackson had a chain of no small extent, including units in Jacksonville, Nashville, Chicago, Shreveport, and Charlotte. Similar chicken chains were aimed specifically at inner-city blacks. Chicken George Chicken and Biscuits, named after the character from Alex Haley's novel *Roots*, was a black-owned chain in Baltimore that spread to thirty-two units in the mid-Atlantic states. Chicago's Chicken Unlimited and Ron's Krispy Fried Chicken, spreading across a smattering of southern states, also did well for a time. Nearly all of these have vanished from the landscape. Some were undercapitalized. Others offered inferior or inconsistent products; some, like the Mahalia Jackson chain, suffered from their ghetto locations being frequently robbed.

A few, like the New Orleans–based Popeye's and the Charlotte-based Bojangles, survive and have carved out a niche for themselves—Popeye's offering a spicy Cajun flavor and Bojangles emphasizing breakfast service. Lee's Famous Recipe Chicken had a royal pedigree, having been founded by the Colonel's nephew, and continues to do business in the Midwest and South. And, of course, all the major hamburger chains, as their menus became ever larger, colonized their sister chains, adding fried chicken to the menu in the form of sandwiches, "tenders," McNuggets, and even, as in the case of Roy Rogers, a full-fledged fried-chicken program.

No chicken-centric rival seriously affected Kentucky Fried Chicken, with one important exception. George Church Sr. opened his first chicken restaurant in San Antonio in 1952, just around the time the Colonel was landing Pete Harman, his first franchisee. Church built a small chain on the idea of higher-quality fried chicken, much as Wendy's would later do in the hamburger business. The chickens were delivered fresh, rather than frozen, to the stores, and were said to be bigger than the standard fryer one might find at Kentucky Fried Chicken. George Church Jr., the hereditary chief of the firm, expanded it aggressively throughout the 1960s and '70s, retaining partial ownership of the stores rather than just franchising them. As a rule in franchise-based businesses, the less active a chain's corporate management and oversight, the greater the potential for franchisees to get lazy and take shortcuts. Fast food, as its name implies, is not a highly prestigious field, and generally most people who work in it, as in every other form of human commerce, are engaged in an involuntary and reflexive life-long calculus to maximize profit and minimize effort. By being a joint operator, Church's was able to impose a level of control Kentucky Fried Chicken could not. Combined with what were believed to be bigger and fresher chickens, it cut into the Colonel's hitherto omnipotent market share. By 1977 the chain had 740 stores in twenty-two states and was coming on like gang-busters, a leader in profit growth not just among chicken joints but among U.S. businesses as a whole.

Against such a formidable challenge, the chances of Kentucky Fried Chicken hewing to the founder's vision was approximately nil, at least under its distant, impersonal over-lords. In 1974 the chain would debut Extra Crispy chicken, a direct knockoff of Church's aggressively breaded, deep-fried product. The Colonel, predictably, was aghast. "Now why did you have to ask me that?" he responded to *New York Times* critic Mimi Sheraton when asked in 1976 about Extra Crispy and Kentucky Fried Chicken's other new products. "They really gag me, that's what I think of them." (On another, equally alarming occasion for Kentucky Fried Chicken management, the chain's founder declared that the Extra Crispy chicken was "a damn fried doughball put on top of some chicken.")[1]

Kentucky Fried Chicken, with so few worthy rivals in its own special corner of the animal kingdom and the idea of overseas expansion still some years off, undertook a series of expensive and futile undertakings. Wall Street had to be encouraged in its belief that the company's early boom years were a template for future growth. So Brown, having no special attachment to chicken, assumed that since people liked Kentucky Fried Chicken, they would also like Kentucky Roast Beef. The Colonel's Beef was launched in 1969. People didn't dislike it, but it had none of the lightning-in-a-bottle electricity of Kentucky Fried Chicken, and after some initial success, the venture collapsed, leaving a hundred stores shuttered. This was likely a blow to the Colonel, who in the early days of his restaurant had been even more proud of his country ham than of his chicken; the ham was a featured dish in the roast-beef concept. Brown also reached back into the Colonel's playbook in starting Colonel Sanders Inns, a would-be motel chain, in 1969. This, too, went nowhere.

The urge to expand should not be dismissed as youthful folly on John Y. Brown's part; even the sagacious Pete Harman, who had more operating knowledge about Kentucky Fried Chicken than anyone, fell into it, purchasing the American franchising rights to a British fish-and-chips chain called H. Salt, Esq., Authentic Fish and Chips. This, too, went nowhere, although the chain survived Harman's investment in it. All these moves presaged what was to be a melancholy motif in Kentucky Fried

Chicken's history: the chain's inclination, demonstrated over and over again, to avoid defining itself by its core product. Roast chicken, grilled chicken, chicken sandwiches, barbecued chicken, chicken tenders, winglets, Rotisserie Gold, and the like come and go on Kentucky Fried Chicken's menu like transient visitors to a youth hostel. They all have met with some temporary success, like the Colonel's Beef, before returning back to the void. The primary product that made the company was renamed "Original Recipe" to make room for the Church's knockoff chicken and never returned to its original place as the titular product served at Kentucky Fried Chicken. Like the Colonel himself, it became more symbol than substance, one part of a larger complex of commodities, indispensable indeed but by no means the essence of the business.

Another aspect of the business that had not been apparent during those bullish early years was the company's less-than-exacting accounting. Wall Street was learning that fast food was not a genie that produced whirlwind profits indefinitely and that the relationships of the company, its franchisees, and the listed profits were not as simple as they seemed at first. The magic of franchise fees was found to give an initial but illusory boost to stock values. All too often the franchisee was a cashbox for the franchising company, a mark who paid through the nose for the right to operate and who was little concerned thereafter. McDonald's was an exception to this practice with its low franchising fees and iron control of operations; but most other chains showed less foresight and paid heavily after the initial fees stopped rushing in.

The one-time payment of a franchisee fee by a would-be operator was a much larger and more short-lived source of revenue than anyone realized at first; basically, it was a big initial payoff for the company that might or might not ever lead to a store even opening. Minnie Pearl Chicken, for example, sold more than 1,800 franchises in summer 1969, but only 161 stores were opened.[2] This disenchantment led to Kentucky

Fried Chicken stock losing over 80 percent of its value within a year of going public, and the trend would become typical of the company's performance.

This was another part of the American Dream that, when followed to its terminus, was less happy than the dreamers imagined. Once they made it, they had to keep making it and in fact could lose everything if they didn't make even more. The pressure never abated, and it was this that twisted the company so far from the Colonel's original vision. It was enormously successful, based on its market share, its profits, its continued growth, and other fundamental economic vital signs—but never profitable enough. Someone always wanted Kentucky Fried Chicken to make more money than it did. Maybe if they sold more Pokemon toys? Maybe if the menu was bigger? Maybe if the food wasn't fried? Various corporate caretakers would be in charge of the company over the next three decades, wave after wave of careerist managers whose primary background and loyalty was to a large corporation rather than to Kentucky Fried Chicken and its founder. Even today, with the most stable and healthy ownership the company has had since the time of its founding, Kentucky Fried Chicken is considered the weak sister of Yum! Brands, its current parent company. And why shouldn't it be? Taco Bell's food costs are negligible and its bean and cheese concoctions little harder to make or more expensive to stock than one might find in a prison commissary. Pizza Hut, likewise, can sell a piece of frozen bread with tomato sauce and industrial cheese for five dollars anywhere it can place an oven and a cash register.

Contrast this with Kentucky Fried Chicken's product, its troublesome carcasses and bubbling oil and unhealthy, déclassé product. David Novak, the CEO of Yum! Brands, was still apologizing for the primacy of a company called Kentucky Fried Chicken being known for fried chicken forty years later.

At KFC, there's no question we have our work cut out for us as some store sales declined 4% during 2009. Unlike the rest of the world where we have a much more extensive menu and a very strong sandwich business, KFC US is primarily a chicken on the bone bucket business. Therefore job number one is to stabilize and grow this segment . . . first we launched Kentucky Grilled Chicken. This product receives rave reviews and now represents around one quarter of our chicken on the bone business. And the fact is, we hate to think where we would be without it given the fact the vast majority of our customers are cutting back on fried foods. . . . we no longer have the "fried" veto vote.[3]

One way to cover up this evil secret, of course, was to rename the company KFC, a ludicrous ruse but one desperately required by a company with a giant market share that needed it to become even bigger. In the United States, where KFC was a mere "chicken on the bone bucket business," average sales were $960,000 in 2009—less than in the previous three years but still almost $1 million per store. It's an astronomical sum, beyond the dreams of cupidity to everyone except the only person who matters: the collective stock-buying public, which likes growth more than either revenues or profits and which punishes past success with a dreaded downward arrow of doom. The stock price drove the product for most of Kentucky Fried Chicken's history rather than the other way around. There has been almost nothing that the business would not sacrifice for short-term profitability, particularly in the decades since Brown sold the company to Heublein in 1970.

To take the most egregious example, if anything was or is sacred to the corporate culture of Kentucky Fried Chicken, if the brand has any value at all other than its ownership of the Colonel's posthumous image, it lies in his most storied relic—the yellowing sheet of paper where the eleven herbs and spices are listed that supposedly constitute his original recipe. An enormous amount of lore surrounds this recipe, from its creation to its various hiding places over the years to the current measures taken by the company to safeguard its priceless identity. In 2010 the company made a very public announcement of the new security system of the kind that world-famous jewel thieves watch with raised brows in caper movies. According to a press release,

> The Secret Recipe's new high-tech home is like something out of a Hollywood movie. The custom-built, digital Fire-King safe protecting the Secret Recipe weighs more than 770 lbs and has a ½" thick steel door. The computerized safe also boasts a dual-opening system that requires both a smart key and a personal identification number (PIN). A built-in silent alarm and time lock feature provide additional layers of safekeeping, which will alert the security team of any attempted intrusion and allow access to the safe only during pre-set periods of time. But the new safeguards don't end with the safe. The vault housing the new safe is reinforced with two feet of concrete in the ceiling, walls and floor to ensure that no one can tunnel or drill into the vault. Additionally, the vault and safe are now under 24-hour video and motion-detection surveillance.

Nor are these the only safeguards. "The recipe is such a tightly held secret that not even [the CEO] knows its full contents. Only two company executives at any time have access to the recipe. KFC won't release their names or titles, and it uses multiple suppliers who produce and blend the ingredients but know only a part of the entire contents."

The only problem is that nobody is really sure that Kentucky Fried Chicken is using it. The Colonel insisted over and over again during his lifetime that it had been changed, that it didn't taste the same, that the new owners were cutting corners. William Poundstone, in his 1983 book *Big Secrets*, claimed that the current version consisted entirely of salt, pepper, and MSG.[4] Many customers maintain that the taste of the Original Recipe today is not the same one they recall from the 1960s and '70s. It's impossible to say, of course, and subjective taste, particularly when time and nostalgia are involved, are notoriously unreliable. The question of whether KFC still uses the eleven herbs and spices, though, is a profound one. Without it the brand essentially ceases to exist, which is one reason the company has been zealously protective of the recipe over the years.

On the other hand, what guarantee is there that the Kentucky Fried Chicken franchises of the John Y. Brown era were faithful to the Colonel's recipe? The original nickel-a-chicken franchisees got their seasoned flour directly from the Sanders kitchen, where it was mixed up and bagged by Claudia and a few helpers. After that, the matter was in the hands of an institution fighting for its survival in one of the most demanding competitive markets in America. Brown, although ingenious, well-meaning, and genuinely loyal to the Colonel, made it explicitly clear that his duty was to the company and its franchisees and stockholders and that the Colonel's culinary standards were not ones he could follow. "Let's face it, the Colonel's gravy was fantastic, but you had to be a Rhodes Scholar to cook it," an unnamed executive told *The New Yorker* magazine in a 1970 profile of the Colonel. "It involved too much time, it left too much room for human error, and it was too expensive." The writer noted, "This attitude is incomprehensible to the Colonel."[5] If that was the attitude of Brown and company, the subsequent owners of the company had even less compunction about price controls.

In the course of researching this book, I hoped to come to a decisive conclusion about the Original Recipe debate, and while I can't claim to have irrefutable proof, I am convinced that the Original Recipe, while still distinctive and delicious, is not in fact the same recipe as served by the Colonel. I base this assertion on two separate evidentiary streams. One centers on samples of the former recipe obtained through friends of Colonel Sanders, compared subjectively to samples obtained from current KFC franchises. More persuasive, though, is the well-attested story of how Colonel Sanders commissioned Marion-Kay Spices of Brownstown, Indiana, to create his spice mixture. This spice mixture, which is still for sale under the name 99X, is indistinguishable in taste to the samples I obtained of KFC's former seasoning. That is, the flavor profile is the same when mixed in the same proportion to unseasoned flour. When not "stepped on" with an overwhelming flour-to-spice ratio, the seasoning is much stronger and more fragrant and reminiscent of what many old-timers insist is the original taste of Kentucky Fried Chicken, a blast from the company's precorporate past. The story behind 99X is that the Colonel, unhappy with the taste of the spice mix then being supplied by McCormick, approached Marion-Kay Spices founder Bill Summers, who is said to have "cracked the code" of the eleven herbs and spices and possibly to have improved it. That was the Colonel's view, in any case, and he is said by numerous parties to have recommended it to franchisees, resulting in the aforementioned suit. What is not in question is that Kentucky Fried Chicken sued Marion-Kay for infringement on its franchising monopoly rights, which led to the discontinuation of the arrangement. Happily for fried-chicken lovers everywhere, however, 99X is still available online. The origin of the name comes from Summers' having tweaked the mix very slightly; it refers to the mix being 99 percent identical to the original with the "X" representing the tweak.[6]

The perceived degeneration of the spice mix was only one part of the general malaise that infected Kentucky Fried Chicken in the '70s. The company, even under Brown and Massey, was only once removed from the Colonel. Though its senior managers didn't come from restaurant backgrounds, they were, in the larger scale of things, middling entrepreneurs who had hit it lucky; they were also southerners and deeply connected to the chicken-eating public in the states where it was strongest. The new owner, Heublein, was an immense and indifferent corporate entity that picked up the chain in passing, dropping it into a portfolio of holdings so deep it made barely a splash.

The first hints of a sale by Brown came in 1970. Brown and company had succeeded beyond their wildest dreams, but the result was not that different from what the Colonel had encountered when his nickel-a-chicken business started to get out of hand. They couldn't keep track of what was going on. At one point the company's managers didn't know how much money was coming through the system or even how many stores it had.[7] A big executive shake-up the previous year resulted in four vice presidents being shown the door and a bean-counting CFO coming on board, followed the next year by repeated heroic defenses of Kentucky Fried Chicken's financial stability by Brown, who used all his oratorical power to underscore what was actually a very robust business despite its absurd overvaluing (and subsequent undervaluing) by stockbrokers. But Kentucky Fried Chicken was no longer a booming regional company; it was about to be acquired by a corporate giant, and there was one man for whom that step was one too many. Harland Sanders, the chain's founder and goodwill ambassador, announced his retirement from the board of directors in August 1970. When asked why, he told the *New York Times*, "I realized that I was someplace I had no place being. Everything that a board of a big corporation does is over my head, and I'm confused by the talk and high finance discussed at these meetings."[8]

There was much to be confused about. The entire system was in disarray, and it wasn't because of insufficient leadership on the part of senior management. No, the fact was that the entity called Kentucky Fried Chicken by the outside world really consisted of two very different bodies whose backgrounds, motivations, and experiences were totally different. The employees of the company were, almost to a man (and they were almost all men), educated professionals—lawyers, salesmen, businessmen, entrepreneurs of one kind or another. They thought in broad terms and planned for future millions. Their experience with drunken customers, rusted frying machines, and grease fires was limited to what they read about in field reports—if they read those at all. As with almost all large restaurant companies, operations was the least interesting department and one that was generally seen only as a means to driving customer satisfaction or some such end. To the franchisee, in contrast, operations were everything. He or she was likely someone who had spent a long time in the restaurant business, who took fifteen-hour work days for granted, whose whole day was spent in a haze of grease fumes and muttered curses, of empty threats against indifferent teenage workers and servile promises to enraged biddies whose mashed potatoes didn't have enough gravy. The franchisees made money from the system and even to some extent identified with it; but they also knew that the system was built on their backs, their labor, and their risk, and they often regarded franchise owners as useless do-nothings or worse.

It was to the franchisee class that the Colonel belonged, which is one reason he was so beloved by the operators (as opposed to the executives, who with some justification considered him a royal pain in the ass). His sentiments and loyalty all lay with his former "family," as he made clear in his 1974 memoir: "My concern is not so much with the high financing that seems to be necessary to keep Kentucky Fried Chicken growin' as it is with the kind of people who are out there in their Kentucky Fried Chicken stores a-sellin' it, and then with the high quality of the product itself," he wrote. "That's what made it a success from the start."[9]

The Colonel had no intention of keeping this sentiment to himself. No sooner had the 1971 sale of Kentucky Fried Chicken to Heublein (seven years after the Colonel sold it to Brown and Massey) been effected than the Colonel began a series of guerrilla attacks on his new employer. First, he announced plans to open The Colonel's Lady's Dinner House, an antebellum-theme restaurant featuring his wife, Claudia, as a stand-in. The Colonel's Lady's Dinner House would serve Original Recipe chicken, a boast to which Heublein, not unreasonably, took exception. When the company reminded the Colonel (who, it will be remembered, owned very little stock) that it had just paid almost a quarter of a billion dollars' worth of stock for the exclusive rights to that product and that it was paying him $70,000 a year to be its goodwill ambassador, Colonel Sanders responded by suing *the company* for $122 million. By some miracle of diplomacy and salesmanship, Brown was able to convince the company's management to settle with the Colonel for $1 million—along with the promise that he wouldn't openly attack or embarrass the company in the future.

He started to do so practically before the ink was dry on the agreement. The Colonel was still mad. He was very old by this time, still alert and still very much himself, but in his mid-eighties and, as everyone knew by now, never one to worry much about speaking his mind, even when young and penniless. Now that he was rich, world-famous, and in a fighting mood, there was approximately zero chance that he would abide by the settlement. But what could Heublein do? There was no Kentucky Fried Chicken without Colonel Sanders. Oh, to have a nice fictional cartoon mascot instead! Oh, to have an Uncle Ben or a Mr. Peanut rather than to be at the mercy of this old coot's caprices! And they couldn't fire him, no matter how much they wanted, because he embodied the brand, and it was the brand alone—as they believed—that was worth paying for. Could they? It wasn't clear. Strong opinions were expressed on both sides of the issue.

So the war continued. In private, both to longtime franchisees and to friends, he openly said how little the company's executives knew about chicken. That much was true: Heublein was a transnational beverage company with no experience in the restaurant business at all. Its attitude toward the chain seems, at least in the early years, to have been to think of it as an ATM machine that would more or less run itself. Stores were allowed to deteriorate, and there was little policing of the way the weaker franchisees ran their stores—a disaster in any fast-food restaurant, where dirt and disorder are inexorable forces held at bay only by the most arduous exertions and constant vigilance. By every measure—sales, consumer-satisfaction ratings, market share—the product suffered.

More alarming still, from the Colonel's perspective, was the candid disregard the new owners had for him. This attitude preceded his misbehavior and, there can be no doubt, helped precipitate the trouble.[10] "The Heublein people didn't really understand or appreciate the Colonel," John Brown would later say. "They were corporate people. They didn't respect what he had done. Didn't know. They were going to cut him out of their ads. They told me they hadn't made up their mind whether they were going to use the Colonel or not."[11] This attitude could not possibly have been wasted on the man himself, who had proved to be preternaturally sensitive, even to the point of paranoia, on that very point. Nothing could have struck closer to home than the threat of losing the fame, so long delayed, that vindicated his entire life and transformed him in a few brief years from failed motel owner into chicken divinity.

The combination of personal pugnacity, Heublein's very real ambivalence about him, and the unmistakable decay in the chain of which he was the symbol brought out all of his rancor. "It's my face that's shown on that box of chicken and in the advertising. It's me that people recognize, and they stop me everywhere I go to complain," he thundered to Brown. "The damn SOBs don't know anything but peddling booze, and they sure as hell don't know a damn thing about good food!"[12]

The situation finally came to a head in 1976 when, during a visit to New York, he stopped into a Kentucky Fried Chicken franchise in Greenwich Village with the *New York Times* restaurant critic, Mimi Sheraton. The Colonel unloaded on the chicken, calling it "the worst fried chicken I've ever seen," but he saved his worst scorn for the gravy, which he said was "nothing more than wallpaper paste."[13] In Bowling Green, Kentucky, a week later, he expanded on this theme:

> My God! They buy tap water for fifteen or twenty cents a thousand gallons and then mix it with flour and starch and end up with wallpaper paste. That stuff is sludge. . . . there's no way you could get me to eat some of those potatoes. . . .

you're just working for a company that doesn't know what it's doing. Too bad, because it gives you a bad reputation.[14]

The unenviable job of responding to this outburst fell to company spokesman Anthony Tortorici, who bungled the situation further by essentially agreeing with everything the Colonel said. "We're very grateful to have the Colonel around to keep us on our toes," Tortorici said, obviously meaning the opposite. "But he is a purist, and his standards were all right when he was operating just a few stores. But we have over 5,500 now, and that means more than 10,000 fry cooks of all ages and abilities."[15] The smart thing would have been to say that the particular franchise was being looked at very closely by a crack team of operational division managers or some such thing; instead, the Colonel's offhand put-down ended up vindicated, confirmed by the very people one would have expected to deny it. Nor, even at this point, could anyone at Heublein summon the will to fire their own trademark. Not to mention the fallout that would surely follow: as John Cox, the new director of public relations, put it, "Do you really want him running around the country with no controls whatsoever?"[16] Score one for the Colonel.

It was not, as some of the Heublein executives thought, mere perversity or spite; it was the thing that had made him what he was, the superhuman grandiosity that had led him to start walking around in a white suit and string tie and calling himself "Colonel Sanders" as a small-town business owner. He, like his franchisees, was temperamentally unsuited to being a paid employee; he had enough chances at being one, enough for two lifetimes, and had failed again and again. It was impossible for him to let go, to be quiet, to relinquish his ownership of the product that defined him, even so late in life. What was he if not The Colonel? And if a reporter wanted to know what he thought of the product that bore his name and image, what was he supposed to say?

The franchisees found themselves in a similar position.

Legally and morally speaking, they had no more grounds for complaint than the Colonel did; it was Kentucky Fried Chicken that had made them rich, the great red-and-white-striped collective whose Kentucky Kremlin directed their chicken production down to the last degree and whose premier gave them at least a borrowed and temporary authority.

On the other hand, what loyalty did they owe to Heublein? The Colonel and John Y. Brown were the ones with whom they had started out, and Brown was now off trying to start a restaurant chain with the unappealing name of Lums, while the Colonel—the Colonel himself!—was openly at war. Nor were their claims against the company to be dismissed lightly. Heublein, everyone seemed to feel, had been an absentee owner when it suited the corporation, standing by while the system fell into disrepair and subsequently attempting to take control of ailing franchises, imposing draconian and arbitrary directives on store managers who knew far more about the business than the corporate executives could have hoped to. Darlene Pfeiffer, a longtime franchisee, remembers:

> They were out of Hartford, Connecticut, and a lot of them were very well educated, and they thought that we were just a bunch of dumb chicken cooks. They treated us like that; certain ways the Colonel had taught us to operate, they'd say, "Oh, that's stupid. You're going to do it our way or the highway," so to speak. So that's when it started, when our corporate leadership began to let us down.[17]

The stores owned and operated by the company, which had been some of the best performers in the system, now were the worst. Heublein sold off hundreds just to not have to deal with them. Most of the top store managers from the Brown era quit or were fired, and there was a general sense that the company had in a few short years, in the words of John R. Neal of the Franchise Advisory Council, done little but "milk the business, run the stores down, and damn near ruin the KFC brand."[18]

The parties were soon reconciled to the new order. The Colonel was invited to a little sit-down in which it was explained to him that if he didn't dummy up, he would lose his million-dollar settlement and his job. This had the desired effect, but only temporarily, and eventually it took the pleas of his devoted secretary Shirley Topmiller reminding him that she was a single mother with two children to support as well as Pete Harman telling him that he was hurting the franchisees who still depended on Kentucky Fried Chicken's good name. These appeals to his better nature, combined with the very real threat of losing his colonelcy, caused him to capitulate and go back to smiling blandly on billboards.

The franchisees were easier to mollify. They had a handful of very specific requests relating to royalties, territorial exclusivity, and the like, and Heublein granted them all in exchange for the franchisees withdrawing their support of an onerous bill then in Congress that threatened to limit the control of franchisees by their granting bodies. Heublein's stock price had taken a beating from its internal war, and the franchisees counted themselves lucky to be able to salvage something from the battle.[19] The bill, predictably, never passed.

The general decay of the chain continued throughout the 1970s with sales artificially buoyed by the introduction of low-priced specials and such menu additions as barbecued spare-ribs. Plenty of money still was coming in from the stores, but these short-term fixes did nothing to address the general disaffection felt by the public as overall sales, especially of chicken, went down. Even with the special products, sales went down 3 percent each year from 1976 through 1978, and profits declined annually by 26 percent.[20]

The Colonel, for his part, had by this point bigger problems on his hands. His race was pretty much run, and yet there was so much yet to be done: so many hands to shake, so many microphones to speak to, so many new friends to make. He had been the most vocal advocate of staying active late in life, even appearing before the Senate Special Committee on

Aging to give his testimony in 1977. Now his health began to desert him. His diabetes, which had been held in check over a few years, began to act up. Cataracts, arthritis, and a general weariness came over him. He had a series of valedictions, elaborate ceremonial affirmations of his importance, on occasions ranging from Derby Day to a visit to the KFC Franchise Convention in Las Vegas. The most moving by far was the dedication of the Colonel Sanders Museum at KFC headquarters, where pictures of his mother, his little brother, and his sister were honored under archival-quality frames. His first pressure cooker, "Bertha," was kept in a special glass case, a treasured relic. Various honorary degrees covered the walls. There was a movie visitors could watch that unspooled the remarkable life of Harland Sanders. A bust, carved by his daughter Margaret, adorned the room.

He continued to travel, to orate, to make appearances as often as possible. But the following year he was diagnosed with leukemia. As it became obvious that the end was not far off, the urge to see the Colonel with their own eyes one more time ran strong among friends and strangers. Even from his wheelchair he reveled in the attention. His last months were spent planning every detail of his legacy. He had a large tomb built at Louisville's Cave Hill Cemetery, with a suitably heroic bronze bust marking his likeness, and he visited it on several occasions, the better to contemplate his own posthumous fame. He contracted pneumonia in November and fought it gamely, lingering on through sheer force of will for another month. He died on December 16, 1980, at 7:30 in the morning.

5

AFTERMATH OF
THE AMERICAN DREAM

The death of Harland Sanders had no effect on Kentucky Fried Chicken as a business. Far from it. The infirm, quarrelsome man with whom Heublein had warred was gone forever; the eternally beaming Colonel of the bucket was now its sole property. The Colonel's image was now the company's to do with as it wished. Thus began the afterlife of Harland Sanders. He succeeded in transforming himself into "the Colonel" so well that his public persona barely shimmered when he himself passed beyond the physical plane. But the image of the Colonel and the business he represented was different when he died than when he began it. And they would continue to change.

How could they not? The country was different. Colonel Sanders already was out of his element in the 1950s, an operetta character in period costume. Now he was doubly removed from that era. America had seen the transformations of the '60s and the malaise of the '70s. Southern gentility as an ideal had been tarnished, to say the least, by the new image of the South as a bellicose and violent place, the home of George Wallace and Anita Bryant. Fried chicken had likewise lost its luster as an image of plenty; rather than a special Sunday meal, it was perceived, at least in its bucket form, as a greasy snack or at best a lazy indulgence more likely to be accompanied by a cold six-pack than a pitcher of sweetened tea. Women were in the workplace and more often single than ever before; Kentucky Fried Chicken sold many boxes of chicken to them, but the image of a family sitting together at mealtime was no longer the norm. And it was for these kinds of gatherings that the dish was particularly suited, while the hamburger, a meal that fit in one hand and was not meant to be shared, emerged as the ideal food for a mobile and atomized nation. Neither were small restaurants, or small businesses generally, the model for success; the modern corporation, which truly arrived in the '50s, had by the '70s exerted a hegemony that it has not relinquished from that day to this one. More than any other change, this would have a fateful effect on the business after the Colonel's death.

The largest change by far, however, was the cultural one wrought by television's central and defining role in the culture. The nation was plugged in, watching the same programs, and becoming more and more united by the shared air stream: packaged culture as a relief from the violent disjunctions of the '60s. Again, this helped Kentucky Fried Chicken's bottom line because fast food was part of TV culture geared to the exhausted masses but also because it gave the biggest advertisers an enormous advantage over smaller rivals. Some places might have made a better chicken than Kentucky Fried, but they surely weren't going to outspend it on TV commercials. At the same time, the need to appear *au courant* and ever-fresh guaranteed that the menu, appearance, or symbol of Kentucky Fried Chicken would not or could not stay the same.

By the time of the Colonel's death, the meaning of his image had changed. In the '50s his dress and title made reference to southern men of leisure of the nineteenth century. Attenuated as this connection was to the America of atom bombs and astronauts, it still held some real sway in the sentiments of the country. The agricultural past, its ceremonial commissions and antique customs, was not then the abstraction it would later become. That America was indeed distant and alien to the 1950s but was still within the living memory of even the middle-aged. The oldest Americans might remember as far back as the Civil War or whose forebears might have spoken to Adams or Jefferson. The country was that young. The Colonel's string tie and white suit make reference only to itself now; he is likely the only Kentucky colonel about whom most Americans know, if they know of Kentucky colonels at all. Likewise, his image as an antebellum grandee makes no more sense in the current context of America than would that of Martin Van Buren in his wig and ceremonial sword. Insofar as he represents anything in these postmodern times, it involves some kind of mid-century big business: fast-food franchises, processed and uniform, multiplying endlessly across swarming suburbs. Like McDonald's, Chevrolet, and a few other American businesses that rely entirely on omnipotent brand recognition, Kentucky Fried Chicken was forged in the '50s, when the country began to assume its modern form. Paradoxically, as he was an image of the nineteenth century to the '50s, Colonel Sanders now evokes nostalgia for that latter time in an era as far removed from it as Eisenhower was from McKinley or *Peyton Place* from *The Yellow Wallpaper*.

On the business side, Sanders' passing came just as Heublein was coming around to his point of view regarding operations. A "recolonelization" program was announced to the press. In 1977 a capable and aggressive executive, Michael Miles, had been brought in to turn things around before the business was ruined completely, and he had acted decisively. Miles did everything the Colonel would have wanted: he underwent a kind of boot camp with Pete Harman in Utah that included such fundamental lessons as how to make chicken and how to serve the public. He put money into modernizing and cleaning up aging buildings. He met with franchisees and promised them that they wouldn't be forced to buy equipment and supplies at a big markup—essentially that the relationship would be more of a partnership and less outright exploitation. Miles cut out the cheap items and nonchicken products that had been metastasizing across the menu, and he announced a return to core competency: "The notion really was to bring KFC back to basics, to throw out all the gimmickry and the over-reliance on price promotion and new products and so on, to take it back to the original recipe chicken."[1] Best of all, one of his first acts was to meet with the Colonel, whom he allowed to vent at length and who, old and marginalized as he was, still had some good suggestions.

The truth was that Kentucky Fried Chicken still survived largely on the strength of the Colonel's Original Recipe chicken. It managed to fight off the threat from Church's by introducing Extra Crispy, but three quarters of its sales still consisted of the same chicken (at least in theory) that conquered the hearts of the chicken-eating public two decades before. It was a hard product to make, especially compared with McDonald's new processed, pressed, chicken "nuggets" in the '80s. But it was KFC's special product, and there was nothing quite like it. So the company made it the centerpiece of its marketing efforts, adopted the slogan "We do chicken right," and swore eternal fealty to the principles of its fallen leader. The initiatives worked, and soon the chain's resurgence was being held up as a near-miraculous turnaround. For more than two years, every month was a little more profitable than the one before it. Heublein's board finally, in an act of long-needed good faith, invested $35 million in new facilities. "Now we know that this is a nuts-and-bolts business, not a quick-trick marketing and advertising business," CEO Hicks Waldron told *Forbes* in 1980.[2] It only took the company ten years to figure that out.

By the early 1980s, Kentucky Fried Chicken was an unqualified success and one of the top earners in Heublein's portfolio. That made it an attractive commodity for other, bigger companies, even more vague entities with equally little relevant experience in either cooking or chicken. One such was the immensely rich tobacco company R. J. Reynolds Industries, which would later merge with Nabisco and become the face of corporate buccaneering in the 1980s. At the time, however,

Reynolds was still a cigarette kingpin with a lot of money on its hands and an interest in making more. Heublein was profitable—why not buy Heublein? So Reynolds did.

Michael Miles, who engineered the whole turnaround that saved the company, was inexplicably sent packing as part of the shakeup. He was replaced as chairman by Richard P. Mayer, the former head of KFC's U.S. operations. The business press wrote a number of adoring profiles crediting Mayer as the primary author of the turnaround and writing Miles out in the best Soviet style.

This was unjust, but the press couldn't be blamed for writing with uncritical enthusiasm about Kentucky Fried Chicken. The chain, one of the most conspicuous and successful businesses in America, had been in a severe slump during the '70s, like so much else in the country. Its fortunes coincided exactly with the Carter-era malaise, following the trend from the boom years of the early '60s into the abyss of the recession that paralyzed the American economy in the '70s. Its resurgence now seemed to be part of the general narrative of patriotic rebirth that was being woven around the pro-business administration of Ronald Reagan. Mergers and acquisitions were easier than ever before, and wondrous new financial instruments to create capital came into being. No company was more at the center of the new vitality than Reynolds, with its massive cash reserves. The behemoth put its new subsidiary in a position to expand beyond the Colonel's wildest dreams.

The mood of KFC's senior management could be characterized at the time of the purchase as gleeful. After years of struggling to extract the cost of a new striped roof from Heublein, KFC suddenly had all the money in the world at its disposal. Even Pete Harman was beside himself. "KFC grossed something like $2.4 billion in 1982 [the first year under RJR]," he later remembered. "Things were really going good. In 1983 we had 4,500 stores in the U.S. and another 1,400 stores in fifty-four foreign countries. Nobody but McDonald's was even close to us."[3]

The business was booming in the United States, thanks to the back-to-basics approach initiated by Miles and his "recolonelization" program. Reynolds supported all of Kentucky Fried Chicken's management moves, including expensive ones like the creation of "franchise managers" who would go around to stores overseeing operations, imparting the latest cutting-edge management techniques, and training servers in the various nuances of upselling. This was all heady new stuff for the chain, enabled by the new breed of manager being turned out by the nation's top business schools, armed with backgrounds in applied sociology, economics, and market analysis—and utterly unencumbered, of course, with real-world restaurant experience.

Its more ambitious undertakings aside, however, the main focus for Reynolds was to get the Colonel's face to beam down benevolently from every corner of the globe—a goal it was able to attain with surprising ease. Kentucky Fried Chicken had been selling overseas for a long time, but that expansion came in fits and starts. An early initiative brought fried chicken to Hong Kong, but the experiment proved a misadventure and was soon shuttered. Kentucky Fried Chicken franchises were operating in Japan, South Africa, and other countries from the mid-1960s onward, albeit with mixed success. Some, as in Brazil, actually followed the original model of Kentucky Fried Chicken's earliest years, adding the signature product to the menus of standing full-service restaurants. For all that, the expansion did not proceed with systematic political clout, armies of managers, or an unbreakable airborne supply chain. Under R. J. Reynolds, Kentucky Fried Chicken became a legitimate colonial power second only to McDonald's in its ability to take root anywhere and bend local tastes in its favor.

In many ways, Kentucky Fried Chicken had it much easier than McDonald's. While the hamburger was a uniquely American food, invented in the United States essentially from whole cloth, chicken is a universal human food. Beginning in antiquity as a South Asian jungle fowl, it is kept and eaten everywhere in the world. The fried-chicken tradition of the American South, with its communal connotations and complicated racial history, may not have meant anything to the citizens of Bahrain or Beijing. But the people there ate chicken, and they ate salt, and they ate fried, crunchy things of varying degrees of spiciness, and so Kentucky Fried Chicken made sense in a way that its burger-based rivals didn't.

And, surprisingly, so did the Colonel. Of all KFC's overseas conquests, none was more important or more lucrative than its China operations. At the time of writing, KFC had 3,500 restaurants in China, generating nearly a million and a half dollars each, with huge profit margins, and many more on the way. Obviously, a lot went right for that to happen. An entire book, *KFC in China*, was written on the subject by Warren Liu, one of the architects of the business. Colonel Sanders, Liu says, was a natural way for Chinese consumers to connect with this alien product.

> In addition to its product advantage, KFC China has benefited from the symbol of its brand, Colonel Sanders. For millennia the Chinese have revered their aged. Respecting and honoring the elderly, a symbol of wisdom and good fortune, has been a virtue practiced by the Chinese over the centuries. During the 1980s and throughout the 1990s, there was probably no more effective brand symbol than Colonel Sanders with his natural white hair and long beard, offering a perception of wisdom, affection, and grandfatherly gentleness. Young children were attracted by the white-haired grandfatherly figure. Parents and grandparents willingly put their trust in the same gentle, grandfatherly figure. KFC's business was boosted by the image of the Colonel.[4]

As so often with great symbols, the Colonel was valuable to KFC China for precisely the same reason as here in the United States: not for what he represented, but for what he didn't. None of the qualities Liu's Chinese customers associated with the Colonel had anything to do with the business, which was in no way either grandfatherly or family-oriented. On the contrary, it was, behind its white-haired face, a wholly impersonal, faceless, disembodied entity with no discernible human identity at all. By this point, KFC in the United States was owned by a company that had no kind of business relationship with Harland Sanders other than as a logo, and KFC in China was one step removed even from that.

When R. J. Reynolds became RJR Nabisco in the leveraged buyout by Kohlberg Kravis Roberts and Company, described in Brian Burrough and John Helyar's 1990 book *Barbarians at the Gate*, its already remote interest in Kentucky Fried Chicken began to weaken even further. As happened with Heublein a decade earlier, there was no real leadership from RJR Nabisco, which was now primarily involved with the price of its own stock. Eventually, as Heublein had before it, RJR Nabisco management decided to unload Kentucky Fried Chicken despite its vast profitability. In fall 1986, RJR Nabisco sold it to PepsiCo for approximately $840 million and moved on. By this time, all parties involved were used to the shuttling of the business from one corporate owner to the other. The new boss, like the old boss, was a vast beverage conglomerate whose experience in the packaging business was held up, weakly, as a sign that unlike the old boss, this one would be true to the roots of the business. "We didn't fit," Mayer said of the erstwhile parent company. "R. J. Reynolds is a behemoth in the packaged goods business. PepsiCo has a major interest in the restaurant business. It's a better fit."[5] The sale went through on October 1, and sycophantic profiles of the new CEO appeared in the business press. "KFC's lack of innovative leadership in recent years should change under PepsiCo," wrote *Nation's Restaurant News* breathlessly. What this meant, as the article made clear, was that the primary decision that turned KFC around—the decision to stick to what the company did best and improve the way it was delivered to customers—was to be abandoned. Apparently, CEO Mayer didn't get the memo. In the same issue of *Nation's Restaurant News* (*NRN*), Mayer, "as important an ingredient in the chain's success in recent years as the 11 herbs and spices," opined about what he thought made the company successful.

> Since joining KFC in 1977 as a marketing executive, Mayer has strived to keep the chicken chain aloof from the menu expansion binge that has swept up virtually ever other fast food feeder.
>
> "In the past few years, people have gone absolutely schitzoid [*sic*]," Mayer commented. "People are groping for new [market] positions. A lot of chains blurred their image by adding so many new menu items."[6]

Meanwhile, elsewhere in the very same issue, a triumphalist feature, "KFC Rules the Roost under PepsiCo's Wing," contained the exact opposite message: "KFC-USA president Donald E. Doyle has said the major shift in the chain's strategy is the aggressive development of new menu items."[7] Right, then! It was clear who would win this argument, if argument it could be called. A couple of years later Mayer, the invaluable man, joined Mike Miles in limbo. There was no past inside KFC's corporate culture; even leadership, such as it was, consisted of various career executives shuttling into and out of the system. The only way to distinguish one from the other was by their names and titles.

Five years after its self-contradicting PepsiCo pieces, *NRN* repeated the imposture with two more contradictory KFC pieces in the same issue. One was on message with a puff piece on the latest suit occupying the CEO's office: "With a master's degree from Harvard University and a career spent largely in giant corporations, John Cranor III is clearly cut from a different cloth than Colonel Harland Sanders," it began, before going through the usual litany of testimonials to the executive's people skills and tough-mindedness. Cranor, it declared, once had a job requiring actual physical labor picking strawberries alongside migrant workers. "I don't pretend that I'm migrant-worker-friendly," Cranor added, lest *NRN* readers think him overly sentimental.

Meanwhile, thirty pages earlier one could find a more credible story indeed—one that told of the war between the company and the franchisees who actually ran the stores and brought in most of the chain's earnings. Unlike John Cranor III, these owners were in fact cut from the same cloth as Colonel Sanders and despised Cranor almost as much as their departed leader would have. Cranor had little regard for the franchisees; he considered them a hindrance to PepsiCo's making free with its new possession. There was a suspicion among some of them that PepsiCo wanted to own the stores outright and had no compunction about playing hardball with its new partners. Darlene Pfeiffer was the new president of the Association of Kentucky Fried Chicken Franchisees, a powerful group that had been fighting management since 1974.

It was a key moment for the franchisees, since the franchisee contract that had been in place since 1976 was overdue for renewal and PepsiCo was dilatory about renewing it. The contract was one of the strongest in the fast-food business, not because Heublein, who granted it, was especially forward-thinking or had any special concern for the actual restaurant operators, but simply because, as a body, the franchisees had been endowed from the earliest days of the company with collective powers that couldn't easily be trampled. The Colonel had seen to that when he sold to Brown and Massey, who, to give them credit, remained eager to work with their operational partners.[8] The franchisees paid a royalty to the company, contributed to national advertising campaigns, and were guaranteed that no one could open another store within a mile and a half. Most importantly, it was part of the agreement that any franchisee's contract, if the restaurant was up to operating standards, would automatically renew for ten more years when the original twenty-year run was up. This last provision, though it had no impact on the running of the business, was an essential safeguard against the tyranny of any future corporate parent. Had the contract been an open negotiation, any franchisee could not have failed to come under the thumb of his or her vast and impersonal overlords, who might have designs on the store themselves. This eventuality was soon poised to pass, and it showed great foresight on the part of the contract's framers to plan against it.

PepsiCo, it was thought, wanted to operate all the stores itself; it wasn't a federation of small-business owners but a transnational conglomerate, and it hadn't paid $840 million so that it would have to negotiate every move with a bunch of chicken cooks. Cranor presented the franchisees with their new contract, which simply eliminated all of their protections. There would be no renewal rights, no mileage minimums between stores, a ten-year extension so gutted as to be utterly impotent, and, for good measure, a higher franchisee fee. John Cranor III walked into the meeting and, for all intents and purposes, told Darlene Pfeiffer that this was the new contract and that she and the rest of the franchisees would take it and like it.[9]

The franchisees thought otherwise. Unlike the Colonel, who had been bought out early and could only bang his cane in frustration, they were still invested in the business. In any real sense, they were the business. They gathered in Louisville to consider their options. It was obvious that they had only one: one franchisee after another pledged unconquerable resolve, and together they agreed to sue.

Standing up to PepsiCo was no easy thing. It cost money— a thousand dollars per store, and not once, but many times. Moreover, the eleven plaintiffs in the suit, including Pete Harman himself, now sixty-six years old, were declared "franchisees not in good standing" by the company and were forbidden to open new stores or buy existing ones. Eventually the ban was extended systemwide, and for seven years the system simply stopped growing. The franchisees continued to fight, however, lining up behind Harman. If the first, biggest, and most powerful franchisee could take the gaff, so could they. His 250 stores were the royalty of the chain, the best run and most profitable in the system, and his moral authority was spotless as well. The lawsuit dragged on. Kentucky Fried Chicken stopped growing as a business. There was now open warfare between its corporate owners and the people who actually ran it. These were dark times, and in the public sphere that was controlled by PepsiCo, the once-proud brand, absent its real-world founder, was to be abased and degraded by its new owners to a distressing degree.

The next six years were some of the worst in KFC history. With business growth stymied at home, PepsiCo turned its eyes eastward, where it would, as its executives imagined, have a free hand in developing new businesses. There, it was thought, the corporation would not need to limit growth to freestanding restaurants; it could do delivery, kiosks in airports and supermarkets, trailers, and other unexplored avenues. By 1991, pretax profits from overseas for the time exceeded those the company made at home. It made sense, therefore, to pour more money into overseas operations, and to this day those markets remain KFC's profit center.

A more sinister development, from the franchisees' point of view, was PepsiCo's ongoing, insatiable desire to gobble up franchises—more than six hundred over the next three years above the significant number of stores it already owned. It wouldn't have taken much for the franchisees to sell out to PepsiCo; they might have made a nice payday, especially the smaller ones who faced an uncertain future at best—and at worst a seemingly endless war with a parent corporation that could easily afford to wait them out for decades to come.

Behind the scenes, however, PepsiCo was growing impatient with the situation. It was clear within the company that the troubles with KFC's franchisees, which was echoed in Pizza Hut and Taco Bell, the other fast-food chains PepsiCo bought and alienated with its high-handed ways, were making the division more trouble than it was worth. It meant to spin off the business and approved a plan to create Tricon Global Restaurants in August 1997.

Anyone, whether inside the company or out, under the impression that a change of ownership would result in a new and more respectful use of the Colonel's image was soon disabused of the notion. Despite now being a more or less independent company for the first time in almost thirty years, the same inexorable, corrupting influences that had led to wallpaper-paste gravy and wars against franchisees were about to be exerted directly against the Colonel's image in what remains the nadir of KFC's relationship with the name and likeness of Harland Sanders.

Someone at Tricon, noting that young people were not as eager to eat KFC chicken as often as they might be, decided that the Colonel needed to be "hip." It might have been a response to faltering market share and the general sense—inevitable, perhaps, but also shortsighted—that the brand needed to become "younger" in order to persist into the sunny future that Tricon projected for itself. For whatever reasons, that fall Colonel Sanders was turned into a cartoon character for TV commercials, and the degradation of the Colonel's image was complete.

In 1999 the company hired long-standing advertising agency Young and Rubicam to create a cartoon version of the Colonel. Though wearing Harland Sanders' white suit and black glasses, the figure looked nothing whatsoever like the Colonel, nor did it sound like him: actor Randy Quaid was brought in to voice the character, giving him a southern accent utterly different from the rural border-state accent the Colonel actually had and that was well remembered by adults who had seen his commercials. (David Kamp, a food historian, said he would always remember Sanders' boast about how the chicken got an "egg warsh" before frying.)

The cartoon Colonel was a frisky figure who danced, skipped, sang, bopped his cane against things for emphasis, spun around with vaudevillian abandon, and generally behaved like a buffoon. The legendary low point of the campaign featured him showing off his hip-hop cred by dancing the Cabbage Patch, an already dated end-zone dance, and yelling "Go Colonel! Go Colonel!" But, in fact, the depravity of the campaign extended in many directions at once. There was the sheer hucksterism of it. "These days everyone's trying to get Nintendo's Pokemon," he tells us in a pitch shoehorned into a popcorn-chicken commercial, itself an awful novelty product the Colonel would have loathed. "So catch a Pokemon beanbag for only $4.99. Ah'm starting my own collection!" There was also a transparent attempt to court urban blacks, having the Colonel say, "The Colonel, he da man!" and dunking a basketball.

On one level the campaign could be defended as part of a nearly universal practice among American retail brands, which are under constant pressure to keep pace with changing culture. Despite the absence of nearly any hard evidence to the contrary, it is taken as an article of faith that a brand needs to seem young and with-it to "stay novel," lest it sacrifice its "viability" or "relevance." Although some of the nation's most successful brands, like Wonder Bread or Mr. Clean, suffer not a whit from having hardly changed seems to have no larger lesson. (Youthful hipness, the most ephemeral of all social qualities, is uniquely ill suited to committee-designed simulation.) If a fast-food chain was going to resist the temptation to remake itself to teen tastes, it should have been KFC. Like a dowager in low-rise jeans, it couldn't help but look ridiculous with its invention of a dancing, hip-hop-flavored cartoon Colonel; but then, it just couldn't help itself. This was, after all, part of the American Dream too: a fluid flow of constant reinvention that, in taking its pursuers far from their roots, sometimes made them over one time too many.

The chain was, it turned out, one of the most insecure of fast-food entities, as had been shown by an equally frantic decision in 1991 to actually change the name of the company from Kentucky Fried Chicken to KFC. One of the biggest brands in the world experienced what can only be called an identity crisis and literally attempted to erase its name. The earlier act of self-negation was bad enough; it wasn't uncommon for people to refer to Kentucky Fried Chicken as KFC anyway, much as McDonald's is sometimes semi-affectionately called "Mickey D's." A more serious violation came in the form of the chain's ongoing attempts throughout the '90s and even the aughts to dissociate it entirely from the core product, fried chicken. This pained the Colonel's daughter Margaret keenly. When David Novak took charge in 1992, she made a point of saying, "Father would have liked him. He came right out and talked about how proud he was and how proud we should all be of our Kentucky Fried Chicken recipe. He didn't try to hide it by saying KFC like the rest of those PepsiCo people."[10] Even today, after KFC has emerged from its fugue state and again embraced both its name and its founder, there are still hundreds of KFC Express outlets in grim food malls around the country where one can't buy fried chicken but only strips, sandwiches, and other simulacra.

While the campaign got some short-term results in overall quarterly profits, the damage to the brand's prestige, already battered by decades of neglect and mismanagement, was unmistakable. A survey by *USA Today* found that only 15 percent of those polled liked the new dancing Colonel.[11] Other critics used the campaign as a way to bash KFC. Mark Schone, on NPR's *This American Life*, began by mocking the campaign ("The erstwhile southern gentleman twirls his cane like Huggy Bear and pimp-limps to the greasy beat of old-school southern funk") and then used that as a way to revile the Colonel himself, calling him "a redneck" with "the last lingering stink of the Old South" on him who needed redeeming by "growing up to be a black man."[12] Many franchisees were taken aback, despite the sales boost, and the Colonel's contemporaries were predictably appalled. "I was personally offended at that," John Y. Brown said. "I didn't think it was right."[13] KFC was flailing wildly around in search of relevance, which of course had the exact opposite effect, and soon (though not soon enough) saw the folly of its way.

In a way, the cartoon Colonel misadventure spoke to the

essential problem that Kentucky Fried Chicken had always faced and would continue to face. The Colonel's image has certain abstract qualities, such as the grandfatherly wisdom it projected to a billion Chinese consumers or the down-home southern image that was its original purpose. But beyond these eminently helpful qualities was the generally unwelcome fact that Colonel Sanders was a real person—altogether too real for KFC management during his lifetime and even by 1993, more than ten years in the grave, an uneasy fit for the new image that KFC wanted to have. It wasn't just a question of the Colonel being dead; Wendy's revived Dave Thomas a few years after his passing but in a tasteful way, paying tribute to his legacy and promising to continue doing things "Dave's way." The difference was that the Colonel had stood for a particular product cooked a particular way, and that product was (it was thought) no longer as appealing to the public. Let's say, for the sake of argument, that it had been of the utmost necessity that KFC sell popcorn chicken and Pokemon tie-ins. Throwing the Colonel's official portrait onto these products wouldn't help sell them; moreover, the incongruity of pairing an elderly, white-haired gentleman with a Japanese fantasy manga game might even have the undesirable effect of making KFC look ludicrous.

Or, to be more charitable, let's say that it was necessary to connect to with-it youths—certainly, this was a real enough issue for any number of its competitors, such as Church's. The Colonel, in his planter's suit, might not be an ideal symbol for such a market. There is simply nothing to be done about it. The Colonel is the Colonel. He alone differentiates KFC from its rivals, and only his transhuman authority keeps the business from becoming completely unmoored. Fast-food franchisees love to speak about tradition because tradition is what they most conspicuously lack; the buildings and menus and design motifs all change from year to year because they have to, lest they fall back into the pack and be lost in what business writer Robert Emerson has called "the endless shakeout" of emerging and expiring concepts. Words like "classic" and "old-fashioned" are fictions as invaluable to fast-food restaurants as testimonials in a Ponzi scheme.

But at the same time, tradition can be crippling: the conventions of the past can deleteriously hold back the innovations of the future and the desperate need of a business to react to what's happening in the market. Xerox is still reeling from its decision to part with what would become the Apple computer operating system because it couldn't see how that would help sell copy machines. In this regard, KFC has been particularly vulnerable for three decades and counting. But there was always the real, live Colonel acting as a "badwill ambassador," holding the owners back, criticizing them publicly and denigrating their efforts to fend off such real or imagined rivals as Church's or Boston Market. In the '70s he felt, and not without some justice, that as the founder and living personification of Kentucky Fried Chicken he should be able to speak freely about its flaws, presumably in the hope of redeeming them. Heublein executives felt that his job should be to look like the guy on the bucket, wave benignly from cars in parades, and generally not cause trouble. But, as noted, that's not who Colonel Sanders was; if it had been, he would have stayed with the Columbusville Chamber of Commerce or Michelin or his gas station in Corbin or the Sanders Cafe; the man Heublein wanted was a man who would take his check every month as Sanders might have been expected to take his Social Security check when he was sixty-five rather than going around in a car promoting a product that didn't exist and using the image of a man who wasn't famous.

It was akin to the difference between fried chicken and popcorn chicken. Popcorn chicken is created from the void, having no bones or skin or fat; it is malleable muscle tissue, a blank canvas on which to paint crunchiness and salt. Chicken on the bone is infinitely more problematic and complicated. The dark meat doesn't cook at the same rate as the white meat, which takes a long time to cook; the parts are all different sizes; it doesn't conveniently disappear once consumed; it certainly can't be easily eaten while driving or for that matter anywhere there's not a huge pile of napkins and a sink nearby for washing hands. Nobody in their right mind, sitting down to create a multinational QSR franchise, would choose chicken. It's inappropriate in every way for a fast-food concept. But nobody sat down to create KFC as we know it today—the red-and-white leviathan that dominates China and whose stock is traded on Wall Street alongside Exxon and General Motors. It started out as a dining room in a gas station in Kentucky. The desire to distance itself from those quaint but constricting roots had been at the heart of PepsiCo's sometimes licentious use of the Colonel's image. And soon the Colonel's creation, the chain's primary product, would be under attack as well.

Because, let's face it. A transnational fast-food empire wouldn't be founded on fried chicken at all. It would likely be some kind of product that Americans could pretend was good for them, like Subway sandwiches. Despite the universal appeal of fried food in general and fried chicken in particular (to say nothing of pressure-fried chicken), fried food by the 1980s was beginning to enter an irreversible decline in prestige. This was a problem, since the business was founded and had pitched itself as the ideal meal for overworked mothers to feed their families. A typical commercial from the early '70s begins, "Every day, all over town, women have a question on their minds. 'What should I serve my family tonight?' And every day, all over town, Colonel Sanders and his boys are cooking up the answer!" Through years of KFC advertising, this is the theme of themes: pick up a bucket and feed your family. "Kentucky Fried Chicken, it's finger-lickin' good, a treat every family enjoys"—so ran a seemingly ubiquitous jingle of 1971. An increasing concern with eating healthily was something KFC was able to shrug off in the 1970s; as the field became more crowded, though, and as Wendy's and other chains began to offer salads and other, healthier fare, the burden of fried chicken became heavier to bear.

As grotesque as the "dancing Colonel" campaign rolled out in 1999 was, it was not the furthest the company strayed from the Colonel's vision, persona, or product. That seems hard to believe, and yet it is so. In 1991 Kentucky Fried Chicken, under discouraging market conditions and the somnolent and shortsighted leadership of R. J. Reynolds, decided not to be Kentucky Fried Chicken any more. Nothing could have been further from the spirit of the chain's founder; and that is why I have saved it for last, to underscore the distance between the man, his image, and the business that controls the image. They are three very different things in constant tension.

The reasons for so radical an act of self-erasure were, in retrospect, trivial. The business was making millions and was, by any standard, one of the most successful food-service businesses in the world—indeed, in the history of the world. But it wasn't the prettiest girl at the party. The hot thing in chicken in the early '90s was broiled breasts. Burger King's BK Broiler was selling a million sandwiches a day. An upstart Latino chicken chain, El Pollo Loco, was tearing up the market, leading every rival in sales per store. A rush of unfried products was therefore fast-tracked through the system: skinless "light and crispy" chicken, a chicken-salad sandwich, a honey-barbecue chicken wing, a roasted chicken, and, of course, a BK Broiler knockoff. The chain threw everything at the development wall to see what would stick; nothing did. The products were tested in units here and there but never caught on.[14] So, inevitably, someone like John Cranor III appeared out of the void, decreeing that Kentucky Fried Chicken thereafter be less associated with fried chicken and increasingly known just as KFC. Purely from a business point of view, this was a reckless and destructive act; it wasted at a stroke brand loyalties that had been built up for more than thirty years of sustained growth. But PepsiCo, KFC's owner at the time, hadn't been around for any of that, and PepsiCo could do what it wanted.

What was amazing about the weakness and hysteria of such a gesture is that it wasn't really based on any kind of marketplace reality. An interested observer might well scratch his white goatee over the blanket assertion that Americans are less interested now than in the past in eating fried foods. It's a documented reality that Americans are fatter, more self-indulgent, and less healthy in their eating habits every year. And yet to listen to the constant refrains of KFC's senior management, from that day to this, one would think that the country was a macrobiotic nation religiously committed to feeding upon brown rice and vegetable proteins.

That will be the day! Throughout the country and particularly in the South, KFC's stronghold, fried chicken is hugely popular. It is fattening; it is unhealthy to a great extent, although less so since KFC abandoned trans fats in 2007. The idea that this would keep Americans of any kind from eating it is patently ridiculous. This fact would not be lost on KFC franchisees, who see the country's fried-chicken-eating habits at close range and rarely voice their unease about the "on the bone bucket business," with or without the latest product release, whether it takes the form of Kentucky Grilled Chicken, the Colonel's Rotisserie Gold, or any of the other fried-chicken alternatives that have been foisted upon an undemanding public over the years.

What concerned KFC, as it was by then known, may have been more cultural than culinary in nature. It wasn't just that fried food was unhealthy; it was downmarket. Kentucky Fried Chicken was, it seemed to many, déclassé. Its slogan in the 1960s, "finger-lickin' good," was the last thing the company wanted its customers to think of; like all fast foods, it wanted to be liked by everybody. It was liked by millions of Americans; but there was a potential objection to it, so it had to be changed. No attitude could be in greater contrast to that of its founder, who spent his entire life doing things exactly his own way and cajoling the world into seeing it his way.

Had the Colonel been alive, he would have pointed out the obvious. Yes, nonfried chicken products were doing well; so were hamburgers. So what? Kentucky Fried Chicken was doing better than at any time in its history, by any measure. None of the new products tried out either by Cranor's administration or his predecessors outsold the Original Recipe chicken; nor had the name Kentucky Fried Chicken failed to attract the hungry in this or any other country under the sun. Despite its unfaltering profitability, the chain was always looked at as a flawed holding in the PepsiCo portfolio; many in senior management didn't even like the brand as much as its sisters, Pizza Hut and Taco Bell—themselves both wildly successful, idiosyncratic businesses that had found their way into the corporate gullet in the 1980s, mostly as a way to keep the chains' taps flowing with Pepsi. Kentucky Fried Chicken was just another division to make over in time for the annual report. "We are dramatically changing our menu, our restaurants and the way customers think of us," said KFC senior marketing vice president Bill McDonald in the press release announcing the name change. "And we wanted our graphics to reflect the new KFC."[15]

It wasn't a case of simple mismanagement or misjudgment; the problem was systemic. There was no founder to demand things be done his way; there was no single person with the authority that had died with the Colonel. John Cranor III was gone from his job by 1994; the man who replaced him, David Novak, would turn out to be the longest-running and most supportive executive the company had ever had. Even as the horrible, paralyzing franchisee lawsuit was dragging on into its fifth year, Novak was able to persuade the franchisees that he was the longed-for executive who would appreciate and support them at last—the loving corporate parent they had never known, other than those few who supped with the Colonel so many years ago. He even told them that he wouldn't leave the job until KFC was on the mend, understanding as well as the franchisees just how little invested previous "leaders" had been.

> When I first became president of KFC, I told the franchisees I wasn't going to leave until we turned the business around. I said it to get them to trust me because they were so used to having corporate guys come in, work for a couple of years, and then move on, so that there was really no sense of con-

tinuity, no sense that the president really cared about the company as more than just a stepping stone in his career.[16]

Even the Colonel's family approved of the dynamic young executive. Novak took the extra step of singling out the Original Recipe chicken for praise rather than the usual blame: "There is nothing that matches the original recipe at KFC. People have tried for years to match it, and they haven't come close. We have over a 50% share in that market, and we should be proud of it."[17] (The suit was settled in 1997, with Pepsi withdrawing its hard-line 1989 contract prior to the spin-off.)

And yet, during both Novak's tenure at KFC (1994–1997) and throughout his subsequent years as the head of Tricon and then Yum! Brands, he oversaw the same depressing efforts to distance KFC from its primary product—and by extension, from its customers and, of course, its famous founder. The point of the new-product frenzy wasn't to make loyal KFC customers happy; they were already happy. That's why they were loyal customers. It was to attract new customers. But there were built-in limits to this strategy, as the Colonel, for all his ignorance of the QSR business, understood. Inevitably, the new products cannibalize sales of the old ones and then hurt operating standards as teenagers are asked to cook thirty different products competently instead of one superlatively. Thus even Novak, the executive with the most sustained and demonstrated commitment to the business in its history, was driven to approve what, in retrospect, were ludicrous claims.

For example, PepsiCo was expecting a lot of the public to forget that KFC stood for "Kentucky Fried Chicken." Or was it? The idea embraced by marketing consultants, then as now, was that young people, the target audience of any fast-food chain, didn't have any associational baggage about the place. To a young person encountering "KFC" as a latchkey child or bawling toddler, there never was another name. But she or he might someday wonder, what does the "KFC" stand for? The company's marketing gurus anticipated this question and began a surreptitious process of trying to implant the phrase "Kitchen Fresh Chicken" into the minds of consumers. Naturally, this crude plan didn't pass unnoticed. Seth Stevenson, the advertising columnist for the popular website *Slate*, wrote about this plan in 2004, asking, pointedly, "What does KFC stand for?"

> [T]he key in this [campaign] is keeping the brand identity strong, straight through the name transition. That's what KFC is banking on as they take those three famous letters, stripped of their meaning 13 years ago, and attempt to reinfuse them with a nearly opposite meaning . . . Will consumers follow again as they're asked to believe in "Kitchen Fresh Chicken"?
>
> Of course we will, if we hear it enough as it blares from our televisions. Branding is at times a delicate alchemy. And at other times it's just spending lots of money. (Like when KFC tried to convince us fried chicken was a health food.) You hammer away at us with your insultingly wrongheaded message until our resistance wears down and we throw up our hands and we accede that yes, we suppose this chicken does come from a "kitchen" of sorts and, OK, by some tortured definition it could possibly be referred to as "fresh." It's all so finger-lickin' sad.[18]

More doomed still was a similar brainwashing campaign, alluded to in his essay, to convince consumers that they could in fact eat plenty of fried chicken because it was actually healthy. Though it may sound surreal now and did even at the time, it's a testament to the power of executive self-delusion that this was actually an official campaign undertaken by the company. "With more and more Americans on diets and increasingly health-conscious," a 2003 press release read, "we thought it was important to get this information to consumers so they can judge for themselves how to make KFC part of their healthy lifestyle."[19]

The commercials were even sillier. In one, a man is seen leaning against a truck, eating a cartoonishly large piece of chicken. "Is that you?" his buddy asks. "You look fantastic! What have you been doing?" (Set aside for the moment the fact that no guy would ever say this to another guy.) "Eating chicken," comes the self-satisfied reply. "The secret's out!" a peppy voice-over informs us. "One Original Recipe chicken breast has just 11 grams of carbs, and packs 40 grams of protein!" In another, a trim and well-meaning wife reminds her shlubby husband, "Remember how we talked about eating better?" He nods. "Well, it starts here!" she says, whipping out a big bucket of fried chicken! The announcer informs us that KFC chicken has less fat than a Whopper—as if anyone ate five or six Whoppers at a sitting, as the seated slug before us is surely poised to do with his bucket of chicken. (A bucket has twelve pieces in it, which would be lucky to get through three quarters of football.)

As bad as these commercials were, the rock bottom of the campaign came buried in the language of the press release itself, which was held up to ridicule in *Slate*. "In a particularly brilliant maneuver, KFC's press release further suggests that you can make its chicken even more healthy by removing the skin."[20] The company, whose whole existence was based on fried chicken and the eleven secret herbs and spices that lay impressed upon its skin, suggested taking the skin off.

Taking the skin off!

If the Colonel hadn't been dead, this surely would have killed him. It was as if McDonald's had suggested throwing the burger away and eating the lettuce and tomato between two slices of bread. No, it was worse than that, because McDonald's had rarely boasted of the distinctive flavor of its burger or for that matter of its taste at all. The ad agency "creatives" who had been put in charge of boosting sales were doing everything in their power to redefine the brand short of replacing Colonel Sanders—and how far off could that be? Reaction was, as always, negative. For the thousandth time, the company was told, as it had been by the Colonel, Pete Harman, the franchisees, the public, and everybody else, that the problem wasn't the marketing or the slogan or who their latest rival was or that the food was fried rather than grilled. The problem was one of bad faith. It was easy for people outside of KFC's corporate culture to sense that those inside that culture were apologizing for the product rather than promoting it.

There were certain realities KFC needed to face. Some people would never eat the chicken because they thought it was nasty and fattening, and the people who did eat it loved it to the tune of $5.3 billion a year in the United States alone. It would never be as cheap as the food at Taco Bell or as easy to make as the frozen pies at Pizza Hut. In any case, the brand anxiety, which continues to vex the chain, only makes it look bad. "If KFC wants me to buy their fried chicken," wrote Rob Walker in *Slate* in response to the healthy-chicken fiasco, "the company should try to convince me that its product is actually worthy of the name. Maybe they considered that idea at some point—and decided that selling the stuff as health food just seemed more credible."[21] Ouch!

More temperate, and more bluntly true, was the sentiment expressed a couple of years later in *Advertising Age*, the widely read trade paper considered the industry bible.

The fast-food chain formerly known as Kentucky Fried Chicken seems to have tried everything. It's changed its name to initials, then back to words, then back to initials. It's leaned on cheap marketing stunts such as moving the secret recipe, taking Colonel Sanders to the U.N. and, most recently, launching the 500-calorie Double Down sandwich, which replaces bread with chicken breasts. . . . the moves also contributed to a lack of consistent brand positioning and a distraction from KFC's flagship product—both of which have hurt the chain and allowed competitors to creep in and carve out share.[22]

The writer had a point but erred in thinking that the only challenge to KFC was in getting properly on message. There was no way to get on message because the message itself was hopelessly conflicted. And the reason it was conflicted was that Yum!, like PepsiCo, R. J. Reynolds, and Heublein, wanted the product to be something it wasn't. The proof of this was the way Novak, for all his expressed faith in fried chicken as the Colonel made it, had fallen into the same quagmire as all his less idealistic predecessors. There was no question that he cared deeply about the company's traditions, about the people who operated the stores, and he felt committed to it to an extent unprecedented in the company's history. Under Novak's leadership, the company would veer back and forth between tradition and new products, between seeing KFC as a great success—which it surely was by any imaginable measure—and seeing it as a faltering problem child that wouldn't go away no matter how many slogans and new products were thrown at it. Yum! meant to honor the Colonel—even going so far as to change his image yet again, his white jacket now replaced with an apron, as a reminder to the world that he was a cook first and a colonel second. Two years later, all that KFC promoters could talk about was its new Kentucky Grilled Chicken, the most successful new product since Extra Crispy, and one that, they hoped, would keep KFC from being such a drag on the bottom line. The response to the Grilled Chicken was warm and resulted in rising sales. But KFC, which was now sold in tripartite storefronts that also offered tacos and pizza, saw sales drop over the next few years as a recession settled in.

It wasn't hard to understand. Not everybody was a KFC customer. Even the young and indigent, upon whom the chain traditionally depended for its life roots, had more choices, many of which were cheaper and easier to consume than Kentucky Fried Chicken in any of its forms. KFC would invariably cost more than either of its Yum! sister brands. It would never seem really young, hip, or healthy. This was demonstrated when in 2006 a scandal erupted over secret footage exposed by PETA, the animal rights organization, that captured unspeakable cruelties being inflicted on chickens at plants that supplied KFC.

KFC fought back strongly, pointing out that it had some of the strongest animal welfare guidelines in the business, that it had an advisory committee that included Dr. Temple Grandin, the nation's leading authority on humane animal treatment, and so on. But there wasn't really any need; the sort of people who paid close attention to PETA or animal rights in general weren't KFC customers to begin with. Still, there was that potential KFC customer, the one who wasn't already contributing to the billions in sales the chain boasted, and it was that customer who received all of KFC's attention and all of KFC's concern.

While understandable from a business point of view, this position was very un-Sandersian. Kentucky Fried Chicken, as KFC returned to being called now and again, would always be, no matter how many millions were expended on marketing and advertising, essentially a specialty product, the inescapable product of its origin at a particular time in a particular place by a particular person. For all its twenty-first-century hypercompetitive, ultrarationalized, globally expansive power, it was at the end of the day a product justly represented by an old man who believed in himself, his pressure cooker, and his recipe for fried chicken.

In the three decades since Harland Sanders, also known as the Colonel, passed away, his image has become more common and less meaningful. In 2006, as part of another image revamp—the one in which the Colonel got an apron—KFC commissioned what it claimed to be the largest mosaic ever built, an 87,500-square-foot Colonel Sanders logo in Area 51 of the Nevada desert, so large that it could, it was claimed, be easily visible from space. The purpose was not to signify to passing extraterrestrials where they might find a good meal, though certainly that was a side benefit. The point was to underscore the vastness and universality of the Colonel's image, to pay homage not so much to him as to the icon he had become. There was something philosophically revealing about the whole experiment: it was a testament to the gigantism of the whole enterprise and how far it drifted from the reality of any one human being. The mosaic was impossible to discern on the ground; it made sense only from ten thousand feet up. In this way it was the perfect image for what had happened to the Colonel, his fame, and sales of his chicken, all of which grew much larger and meant much less than anyone could have predicted.

Yet this transition could only have happened after his death. The youthful public, polled in 2010, was woefully ignorant in thinking that Colonel Sanders was not a real person. Had he not been, the contrast between his identity and his image, his violent temper and hot-blooded fits of anger, and the cool, dispassionate, and reckless way he and the company he founded were treated by the corporations for so many years would not be so poignant. The Colonel, whose ambition knew no bounds and whose stubborn, ineradicable sense of self survived even his own apotheosis, did in fact live the American Dream. He transcended his own limitations and the conditions of his birth. But in retrospect, it was his greatest triumph, and his best legacy, that he didn't transcend them completely. He continues to represent a very real time, place, product, and person, and his icon is hollow without the man behind it.

≡ NOTES ≡

Introduction

1. "KFC Tries to Revive Founder Colonel Sanders' Prestige," *USA Today*, September 9, 2010.

2. James Truslow Adams, *The Epic of America* (Boston: Little, Brown, 1931), 404.

Chapter 1

1. John Ed Pearce, *The Colonel* (New York: Doubleday, 1982), 7.

2. Ibid.

3. Don Ledington, interview with the author, Lexington, KY, April 20, 2010.

4. In Pearce, *The Colonel*, 21.

5. Ibid., 107.

6. C. Wright Mills, *White Collar* (New York: Oxford University Press, 1951), 182.

7. Pearce, *The Colonel*, 31.

8. John Y. Brown Jr., interview with the author, April 20, 2010.

9. Harland Sanders, *Life as I Have Known It Has Been Finger-Lickin' Good* (Carol Stream, IL: Creation House, 1974), 43.

10. Harland Sanders, *Life as I Have Known It*.

11. "Poultry Slam 1999," *This American Life*, WBEZ, November 26,

1999. http://www.thisamericanlife.org/radio-archives/episode/145/
poultry-slam-1999.

12. "Kentucky Town Re-Examines Its Racial History," NPR,
March 10, 2007. http://www.npr.org/templates/story/story
.php?storyId=7772527.

13. Pearce, *The Colonel*, 51.

14. Ibid., 53.

15. Margaret Sanders, *The Colonel's Secret* (Wellington, FL: Ibis
Foundation, 1988), 101.

16. Duncan Hines, *Adventures in Good Eating* (Bowling Green, KY:
published by Duncan Hines, 1935), 89.

Chapter 2

1. In Pearce, *The Colonel*, 86.

2. Ibid., 50.

3. In Philip Langdon, *Orange Roofs, Golden Arches: The Architecture of American Chain Restaurants* (New York: Knopf, 1986), 30.

4. In Edward G. Klemm Jr., *Claudia: The Story of Colonel Harland
Sanders' Wife* (Los Angeles: Crescent, 1980), 423.

5. R. David Thomas, *Dave's Way* (New York: Berkeley Books, 1991),
57–61.

6. Harland Sanders, *Life as I Have Known It*, 98.

7. Calvin Trillin, *The Tummy Trilogy* (New York: Farrar, Strauss,
and Giroux, 1994), 332.

8. Robert Darden, *Secret Recipe: Why KFC Is Still Cookin' after 50
Years* (Irving, TX: Tapestry Press, 2002), 41.

9. The Colonel would dispute this late in life, claiming, "I built
Kentucky Fried Chicken, not on the name of Colonel Sanders'
Chicken—I could've used that just as well—but I chose the romance
and the love and the historical name of Kentucky to add to the product. I figured it would carry better worldwide than it would be to look
like an ego on my part, to say it was my chicken." The first commercial
use of the name, however, was at Harman's Salt Lake City store. "Fri-
day Flashbacks: Tribute to Colonel Sanders," WHAS-11 (Louisville,
KY), November 20, 2009, video. http://www.whas11.com/home/
Friday-Flashbacks-Tribute-to-Colonel-Sanders-70657897.html.

10. In John L. Crawford, *It Wasn't All Gravy* (Louisville, KY: KFC
Corp., 1981), 2.

11. Ibid., 6.

12. In Darden, *Secret Recipe*, 44.

13. Pearce, *The Colonel*, 114.

Chapter 3

1. Frederick C. Klein, "John Y. Brown, Rich and Taking It Easy," *Wall Street Journal*, April 1, 1975.

2. Brown, interview.

3. Ibid.

4. Ibid.

5. In Pearce, *The Colonel*, 125.

6. Harland Sanders, *Life as I Have Known It*, 126.

7. "Harland Sanders Is Dead at Age 90," *Louisville Times*, December 18, 1980.

8. Brown, interview.

9. Margaret Sanders, *Colonel's Secret*, 325.

10. In Darden, *Secret Recipe*, 84.

11. Brown, interview.

12. In Pearce, *The Colonel*, 137.

13. Brown, interview.

14. Darden, *Secret Recipe*, 104.

15. Ibid., 149.

16. Ibid., 149–150.

17. Ibid.

18. Margaret Sanders, *Colonel's Secret*, 325.

Chapter 4

1. Mimi Sheraton, "For the Colonel, It Was Finger-Licking Bad," *New York Times*, September 9, 1976. "Col. Sanders Is Cleared of Libeling Restaurant," *Washington Post*, March 15, 1978.

2. "Franchising: Too Much, Too Soon," *Business Week*, June 27, 1970, 54.

3. Yum! Brands 2009 Annual Report, 8.

4. William Poundstone, *Big Secrets: The Uncensored Truth about All Sorts of Stuff You Are Never Supposed to Know* (New York: Morrow, 1983), 20–21.

5. William Whitworth, "Kentucky Fried," *New Yorker*, February 14, 1970, p. 40.

6. "The Visit," *What Is Cooking.* http://pinesponderings.com/?p=14.

7. "Franchising," *Business Week*, 55.

8. "Colonel Sanders Bowing Out," *New York Times*, August 8, 1970.

9. Harland Sanders, *Life as I Have Known It*, 131.

10. Darden, *Secret Recipe*, 119.

11. Brown, interview.

12. In Darden, *Secret Recipe*, 121.

13. In Sheraton, "For the Colonel."

14. In Pearce, *The Colonel*, 199.

15. In Darden, *Secret Recipe*, 122.

16. Ibid., 124.

17. Darlene Pfeiffer, interview with the author, November 15, 2010.

18. "Power to the People," *QSR Magazine*, September 2000.

19. Darden, *Secret Recipe*, 132.

20. "Chain's Fortunes Improved When It Rearticulated Its Mission and Strategic Plan," *Marketing News*, July 9, 1982, p. 14.

Chapter 5

1. Darden, *Secret Recipe*, 136.

2. "The Education of Hicks Waldron," *Forbes*, December 8, 1980, p. 98.

3. In Darden, *Secret Recipe*, 160.

4. Warren K. Liu, *KFC in China* (Singapore: John Wiley and Sons, 2008), 69.

5. In Darden, *Secret Recipe*, 170.

6. "Mayer a Key Ingredient in KFC's Successful Formula," *Nation's Restaurant News*, December 15, 1986, p. F8.

7. "KFC Rules the Roost under PepsiCo's Wing," *Nation's Restaurant News*, December 15, 1986, p. F3.

8. Darlene Pfeiffer, interview with the author, November 3, 2010.

9. Ibid.

10. In Richard L. Papiernik, "David Novak: The Pizza Hut/KFC Quarterback Builds a Better Team on His Drive to a Fast-Food Touchdown," *Nation's Restaurant News*, January 1997.

11. "New Colonel Misses Beat," *USA Today*, July 12, 1999.

12. "Poultry Slam 1999," *This American Life*.

13. Brown, interview.

14. "Getting Burned by the Frying Pan," *New York Times*, March 20, 1990.

15. "KFC Shuns 'Fried' Image with New Name," *Nation's Restaurant News*, February 25, 1991.

16. David Novak, *Adventures of an Accidental CEO* (New York: Crown, 2007), 107.

17. In Papiernik, "David Novak: The Pizza Hut/KFC Quarterback," *NRN*, p. D2.

18. Seth Stevenson, "What Does KFC Stand For Now?" *Slate*, May 3, 2004. http://www.slate.com/id/2099747.

19. In Rob Walker, "Chicken-Fried Bull," *Slate*, November 10, 2003. http://www.slate.com/id/2090861. The press release was removed, wisely, by KFC.

20. Ibid.

21. Ibid.

22. Emily Bryson York, "KFC's Stunts Make Nightly News but Don't Stop Sales Slide," *Advertising Age*, April 19, 2010, p. 1.

≡ INDEX ≡